Praise for Meg Keene and
A Practical Wedding

"The Bible of all wedding reason."

—*Huffington Post*

"Fortunately, the person taking emails at A Practical Wedding has the patience of a saint when it comes to the privileged and entitled (a quality that I would also like to possess, but my doctor continues to refuse refilling my Ativan)."

—**Jezebel, I Thee Dread**

"Keene's wedding planning guide is a fresh, sane voice in a field of guides pushing big budget weddings."

—*Library Journal*

"Keene offers couples of all faiths, ages, budgets and sexual orientations a wise and well-written hands-on guide for navigating the complexities of etiquette and cultural expectation. (Five Stars)"

—*Portland Book Review*

"Sure, Pinterest boards are a fantastic wedding resource. But, how can you transform those beautiful photos into a reality? Keene helps engaged couples do just that. From its practical charts and spreadsheets to its fluff-free suggestions, this planner is one you'll want to make your dreams come true (within your budget)."

—**Brit + Co**

"Expect a big-hearted, broad-minded, super smart low-down on the indispensable practicalities of getting married."

—*BookPage*

A PRACTICAL WEDDING

Second Edition

Also by Meg Keene

A Practical Wedding Planner

A *Practical*
WEDDING

Second Edition

Creative Ideas for a
Beautiful, Affordable, and
Stress-Free
Celebration

MEG KEENE

LIFE
LONG

Da Capo Lifelong Books
Hachette Book Group
1290 Avenue of the Americas, New York, NY 10104
HachetteBooks.com
Twitter.com/HachetteBooks
Instagram.com/HachetteBooks

Printed in the United States of America

Second Edition: December 2019

Published by Da Capo Lifelong Books, an imprint of Perseus Books, LLC, a subsidiary of Hachette Book Group, Inc. The Da Capo Lifelong Books name and logo is a trademark of the Hachette Book Group.

The publisher is not responsible for websites (or their content) that are not owned by the publisher.

Print book interior design by Amy Quinn.

Library of Congress Cataloging-in-Publication Data
Names: Keene, Meg, author.
Title: A practical wedding: creative ideas for a beautiful, affordable, and stress-free celebration / Meg Keene.
Description: Second edition. | New York: Da Capo Lifelong Books, 2019. | Includes bibliographical references and index.
Identifiers: LCCN 2019030828 (print) | LCCN 2019030829 (ebook) | ISBN 9780738246727 (paperback) | ISBN 9780738246734 (ebook)
Subjects: LCSH: Weddings—Economic aspects. | Weddings—Planning.
Classification: LCC HQ745 .K44 2019 (print) | LCC HQ745 (ebook) | DDC 395.2/2—dc23
LC record available at https://lccn.loc.gov/2019030828
LC ebook record available at https://lccn.loc.gov/2019030829

ISBNs: 978-0-7382-4672-7 (trade paperback), 978-0-7382-4673-4 (ebook)

LSC-C

10 9 8 7 6 5 4 3 2 1

For my dad, who was my biggest cheerleader

The wedding was very much like other weddings, where the parties have no taste for finery or parade; and Mrs. Elton, from the particulars detailed by her husband, thought it all extremely shabby, and very inferior to her own. "Very little white satin, very few lace veils; a most pitiful business!" . . . But, in spite of these deficiencies, the wishes, the hopes, the confidence, the predictions, of the small band of true friends who witnessed the ceremony, were fully answered in the perfect happiness of the union.

—Jane Austen, *Emma*

Getting married is an attempt at turning air into matter, transforming the ineffable workings of the heart into things that are "real": the invitation, the dress, the ring. The words that constitute a wedding are magical incantations of the highest order. In the presence of witnesses and voiced by a vested authority, two people are pronounced a single unit. Ta-da!

—Anita Diamant, *Pitching My Tent*

You get to a point where there's not much you can do but put on your fancy party dress and a pair of fabulous shoes and grab a bottle of cheap champagne to swig with your girls on the way to meet your person.

—APracticalWedding.com comment

Contents

Preface

I first wrote this book in 2011. You might remember this as the Time Before Pinterest Exploded. But for me, it was a year and a half after our wedding, and I had been publishing APracticalWedding.com for three years. At the time, the wedding industry was in a terrible moment. I mean, it's the wedding industry. It's never really been a beacon of sanity or progressive values. But 2011 was a particularly dark time. We were coming out of the depths of the Great Recession, but every wedding publication in existence assumed that people getting married had piles and piles of money to spend, a professional wedding planner, and a baseline desire to look like a puffy white cupcake. They also insisted on constantly using the phrase "Your Big Day," a term that made me upset then, and still makes me upset now.

I wrote this book while simultaneously riding the high of our amazing wedding and feeling enormous rage at the wedding industry. Apparently, I was far from alone. When I first pitched this book, publishers told me nobody would want to read it. The brides publishers imagined—and they never imagined anyone but brides—wanted binders filled with endless lists telling them how to have a huge wedding where they could feel like princesses. (Were they imagining brides, or confusing them with four-year-olds? It remains unclear.) But with more than one hundred thousand copies of my books sold, and countless dog-eared pages passed from hand to hand, we can now prove that they were wrong all along. All of which gives me the opportunity to update this book for today's (still kind of terrible, but now with different issues) wedding industry.

Over the past eleven years, I've stayed on as editor-in-chief of APracticalWedding.com, which has gone from a blog being written at my kitchen table to one of the largest wedding publications in the English language. I've been quoted in the *New York Times,* on NPR, on BuzzFeed, and, well, in pretty much any major publication you can think of, on how to have a reasonable wedding. I even wrote a second book called *A Practical Wedding Planner* (which you should get because it has all the detailed wedding information you desperately need, but that no one else wants to provide). In short, in the years since I wrote this book, I've gone from a person who writes about weddings to a professional wedding expert.

Coming back to this book as a bona fide wedding expert has been an interesting experience. In this edition, I've worked to share my hard-earned knowledge of why the industry is such a hot mess. But more than that, I've tried to provide you with tools to circumnavigate that (or to at least be firm in the knowledge that you're the reasonable one). I've also updated it to reflect the way the wedding industry has improved—because, believe it or not, things are getting better. These days, you no longer have to struggle through buying a bridesmaid dress in white to get an affordable wedding dress, because there are major retailers that sell exactly that (with free returns). I like to joke that in my day, you used to have to walk uphill to your wedding in the snow, and these days you can ride your quirky bicycle built for two in your hip wedding jumpsuit, singing all the way.

And that's kind of true. But the unfortunate downside is the enormous pressure put on couples to personalize every single aspect of their wedding. Now you can't just wear a puffy white cupcake dress; you need a super-personalized wedding outfit that reflects your authentic personal style and says something profound about your relationship. That pressure to hyperpersonalize is really the same as the pressure to have a cookie-cutter wedding, just in a different form. It means more work, more money, and even more pressure to seem relaxed and chill, like you're doing it all without breaking a sweat. Spoiler alert: doing it all while appearing to expend no effort has never been a good look on anyone.

Beyond that, the wedding industry still has so many blind spots. It focuses on white, straight, thin, gender-conforming, able-bodied, wealthy women. That means if you don't fit that mold, it can be hard to find the resources you need to have an amazing wedding that reflects who you are.

While writing the second edition of this book, I reached out to tons of my favorite people to talk about those very experiences, with the hope that it makes every single human who picks up this book feel less alone.

Because you, the person holding this book right now, you are going to have a wedding that is amazing and exactly what you need it to be. In the pages of this book, you'll get to figure out precisely what kind of wedding you and your partner want, and then how to make that happen . . . with as few tears, fights, and credit card applications as possible.

Let's make some (wedding) magic.

Meg Keene
Oakland, CA
2019

Introduction

What Really Matters

Here is what everyone fails to mention before your wedding: Getting married? It's huge. It's bigger than you ever expected or imagined. It's life-changing. And having done it, I can categorically say that it is not about the cute cake, or the glamorous dress, or the luscious flowers (though each of those things can be really fun). It's not even about the beautiful ceremony site or the packed dance floor. It's about something more monumental than all of that. It's about the look on your partner's face as you walk down the aisle. It's about that moment when you exchange rings and somehow transform love into matter. It's about how vowing to care for your partner for the rest of your life, in front of a group of witnesses, subtly changes you. It's about seeing your most unsentimental friends openly cry. It's about the feeling that sweeps over when you fully realize that you have so many people you love in the same room at the same time (or a handful of people you love the most circling you in the courthouse), and that they are all there to celebrate the massive commitment you are making.

A whole industry is set up to sell you a beautiful wedding; it's set up to sell you how things will look. But what matters on your wedding day, what you will remember until you are old and gray, is how it felt. The carefully crafted details are, in the end, just that: details. They barely hit your radar screen on your wedding day. The things that stick with you are those that you could never ever plan. For me it was the four-year-old daughter of our lifelong friend who dressed herself in bright red cowboy boots and an enormous pink hair flower; the wedding dress from the 1950s that I stumbled on in a vintage shop at the last minute; my husband's oldest friend holding my bouquet while I put on my makeup; feeling our lives intertwine as we circled each other under the huppah; laughing as everyone shared stories.

But as wonderful as the wedding can be, planning it is one of the most complicated and loaded processes of modern adulthood. Getting from newly engaged all the way to your wedding day while staying sane and solvent sometimes feels impossible. The process of negotiating things like faith, money, family, and tradition, all in a very public way, would be difficult in the best of circumstances. When you add the enormous cultural pressures of the modern wedding, you can get something akin to disaster.

I assume that if you are reading this, you are probably engaged. That means you are in one of two places. You're in the first stages of bliss and excitement: Whole life together! Wedding to plan! Sparkly new ring (perhaps)! Or you've moved on to stage two—where you realize that planning even a sensible wedding is going to cost two to three times what you expected, and going to take five to ten times the effort that it reasonably should. Oh. And then there are the expectations. The endless, conflicting expectations.

A cursory glance at a wedding magazine or etiquette book will give you an idea of where the expectations are coming from. First of all, there are the lists. Every book or wedding magazine has *lists*—lists ordering that you immediately do *this*, lists forcefully suggesting that maybe you should start doing *that*, mile-long lists of activities that you need to complete if you want to be a Proper Bride. Worse, these books claim to have both etiquette and tradition on their side (they have neither, but we'll come back to that), which ends up making you feel more than a little inadequate and crazy.

The average wedding planning book will talk you through everything you ostensibly need to know, in mind-numbing, illustrated detail. It will talk you through your fabric choices for wedding dresses (which is fascinating until you realize that, although gainfully employed, the only wedding dress material you can actually afford is inexplicably a poorly manufactured polyester—even though you were pretty sure what you needed to have was French lace). It will talk you through what kind of chairs (or chair covers) you need, every flower that you must know before you pick out your centerpieces, and generally all the things that Must Be Done or everyone will be Horribly Offended.

If the expectations ended there, we would be more or less fine. Half insane, but generally fine. Wedding websites can be ignored; charlatans selling monogrammed favors under the guise of etiquette can be scoffed at. But the problem is, expectations run so much deeper than that.

First of all, and most simply, there are our own expectations. After years of seeing weddings with lines of matching bridesmaids, piles of expensive food, and all-night dance parties, most of us have a small outline in our heads of what we want: a silk wedding dress, letterpress invitations, pretty flowers, good food, and a wonderful party. That's not so hard, right? This won't be that expensive, right? Well. If only.

Then there are the expectations of our parents. Our parents want things. They want reasonable things. They want to see us tremendously happy. They want to not be embarrassed when they invite friends, whose children's lavish weddings they have been attending for years. They want to look like a happy and normal family at this, the pinnacle of public family life. The problem is that "normal" and "not embarrassing" in Wedding Land have come to look a lot like a banquet room at the Ritz and a slowly melting ice sculpture . . . that, and a giant wad of cash you no longer have.

And finally there is Everyone Else. Unless you have thrown a wedding or had a baby, you have not met Everyone Else. All those neighbors and coworkers and people at the post office? Before, they were just people we saw sometimes. Now they are our Greek chorus. "Let me see the ring! Ooooohhh, it's big! You must be thrilled!" "How many bridesmaids are you having and what are they wearing?" "What are your colors? You have to have colors!" "Now, try not to spend a down payment on the wedding dress, little lady, no matter how much you want to." "Aren't grooms the worst? They just can't help out to save their lives!"

The problem with expectations is not the sentiment behind them. People genuinely love weddings, want to see you happy, and want to *chat* with you about it (God bless them). The problem is when expectations slowly strip you of your capacity to do anything other than what is prescribed. And what is prescribed tends to be massively expensive and stressful enough to give you a need for mood-altering drugs or a hankering for a nightly whiskey.

But here is the kicker: everything we're being sold as What We Need to Do for Tradition's Sake has little to nothing to do with the kinds of weddings our grandmothers had or, more dramatically, that our great-great-grandmothers had. One hundred fifty years ago, most Americans were still getting married at home, in their parlor, in their best dresses, holding a prayer book or an embroidered handkerchief. One hundred years ago, most weddings had moved to the church, with only some brides wearing white, and the union was often celebrated by a tea party or a wedding breakfast. As for our grandmothers' era? Well, my grandmother took a taxi from Alabama to California at the end of World War II, since the trains were not running for civilians, and got married as soon as my grandfather was released from a Japanese prisoner-of-war camp. She wore the one white satin dress she could find in the store, and her attendants were the nurses from the naval hospital where my grandfather was being treated. Other than the white dress, the cake, the flowers, the vows, and the ring, there is next to nothing in modern wedding traditions that my grandmother would recognize, let alone approve of.

How do we plan a modern wedding while keeping our souls and our sanity intact? I suggest that we do so thoughtfully, and carefully, with an eye to both actual history and tradition, as well as to our relationships. In the past twenty years, weddings have become shockingly homogenized. The list of musts has grown longer and longer, threatening to take both the couple and their finances down with it. If we scale back to the level of formality and expense that our grandmothers and great-grandmothers would approve of, and then add and subtract from there, we might make it through alive, and we will have a better chance of remembering what this party is about. That, and we'll have the iron-clad justifications of actual history, and actual tradition, on our side.

So, here is a love song to the sensible wedding, the joyful wedding, the unbelievably fun wedding. Here is to the repopularizing of the courthouse wedding, the backyard wedding, the at-home wedding, the picnic wedding, the punch-on-the-church-lawn wedding. Here is to weddings that are both simple and stylish. Here is to figuring out what you actually want, and then having the guts to stick to it. Here is a handbook to get you to the other side, solvent and sane. Here is a how-to guide to get your wedding back to basics: a fantastically fun party to celebrate the day on which you start your marriage.

Because the real point of your wedding day is to end up married. Married, with grace.

Meg Keene
San Francisco, CA
2011

{ 1 }

Getting Started

⁓ BEYOND THE SPREADSHEETS ⁓

So much of wedding planning is devoted to the practical details: things that need to be planned, organized, and cataloged in spreadsheets. But what makes wedding planning hard isn't the logistics—or at least not *just* the logistics. It's all of the emotional issues that come up in between the tasks on the to-do list. If you're ready to tackle and master your to-do list, pick up the companion book to this volume: *A Practical Wedding Planner*. But in this book, my goal is not just to give you a grasp of the logistics. Here, I'm hoping to offer emotional wisdom to guide you in this process, wisdom that comes both from my expertise and from the experiences of many humans who have tread this path before you. This knowledge will likely never make it onto a spreadsheet, but it doesn't make it any less important.

As you begin this journey, here is what you need to remember:

(continues)

1

- Take some time to enjoy being engaged before you plunge into the roller coaster of wedding planning.
- Remember the joy. Your wedding celebrates a truly wonderful, life-changing event. So if something isn't making you happy? Chuck it. Learn how to say "no" to what you don't want and "yes" to what makes you grin.
- Engagement is a transition. It's a time when you get to figure out how to work with (and sometimes fight with) your partner and your extended families about really big issues. On a bad day, this can feel like some of the highest-stakes interpersonal negotiating you've ever had to do, but it's important practice for all the big life decisions to come.
- Consider some form of premarital counseling, even if it's just the two of you sitting down over several evenings and discussing the list of relationship and life questions provided in this chapter. Wedding planning is about planning for one day. Don't forget the marriage planning, which is planning for the rest of your life.
- As you start the planning process, brainstorm with your partner to come up with a wedding mission statement, which will guide you throughout this process.
- Remember many of the wedding images you see online are created by a team of professionals and are an idealized, styled, professional image of what a wedding can look like . . . not the IRL messy, imperfect thing.
- Figure out what your wedding nonnegotiables are before you talk to your family, and, if you need to, be firm with them that these items are off the table for discussion.
- Ask and really listen to what your families' needs are for your wedding.
- It's not your day—it's everyone-who-loves-you's day—but it is your wedding. Let this shape your compromises (and do make compromises).

Here We Go . . .

You've just gotten engaged! You're thrilled, your families are thrilled, and your friends are giddy for you. So, what should you do next? Well, nothing. Nothing except tipsily sip champagne and passionately kiss your partner. Take some time to enjoy being engaged. Celebrate.

When people start asking you about the wedding, tell them, "Oh, goodness, we're just so excited to be engaged, we haven't even thought about that yet." Then, when you've spent at least two weeks enjoying the feeling of glee and bliss, you're ready to start the planning process . . . slowly.

In this chapter, I'll walk you through the first steps: finding your way through the process of being newly engaged, dreaming up ideas for your wedding, and then slowly aligning those dreams with reality (without losing any of the joy). If you learn nothing else from wedding planning, my wish for you is that you learn to say "yes" to what makes you happy and a kind but firm "no" to things that are wrong for you. And if you can remember during this whole planning process that all you really need is the man, the preacher, and the dress (or the woman, the officiant, and the stylish pantsuit)? Well, you'll be halfway to wedding peace already.

Joy: Yes, It's Fundamental

I know what you're thinking: joy? This is the first subject in a wedding planning handbook? Yes, my friends, it is. Because joy—full-throated, fully present, vibrating joy like you've never felt? That is what your wedding is about. That is the "why" in this planning process, and that is always, always the goal.

While our wedding day wasn't the best day of my life (nor was it perfect), it was one of the great joys of my life. When I showed up on my wedding day, I made the conscious decision to let everything go and just be as present as I could be (we'll discuss how to actually pull this off in Chapter 8). In almost every single wedding picture, I'm grinning my head off. Britta Nielsen, who married on family property in Washington State, described her wedding this way: "There was dancing and 'Bohemian Rhapsody' and fireworks. I saw nothing but grins in every direction. I'd be hard pressed to think of a happier day." When you look back at your wedding, you'll want to remember how happy you both were. You won't care too much about how the details looked; you'll care about how you felt. So, it's important to focus your planning on things that will make you a nonstop-grinning ball of happiness.

Yet somehow, in the world of weddings, very little ink is spilled on joy. We see a lot of pictures of the couple looking beautiful, and the decorations looking quirky and artful, but very few pictures that show the two people getting hitched with heads thrown back, grinning, eyes twinkling with delight. Anna Plumb, who married her scientist husband outside of a rock and minerals museum near Portland, Oregon, told me, "Before we got married, I thought that I would sob my eyes out during the ceremony, but mostly I laughed. Almost all of our photos show my mouth wide open in laughter or the two of us grinning like idiots at each other." While it's impossible to know if you'll laugh or cry during your ceremony, you should focus your planning on things that make you feel delighted and alive. Because if what you are able to give your guests is yourself in your purest form, if you are able to lead them by joyful and relaxed example, then you are giving them the greatest gift you can give. Your wedding will be one for the history books—not because it was the prettiest party that anyone has ever seen, not because you played by all the rules and hit every single mark, but because it was so real, so true, so indescribably full of joy.

Remember what your wedding is: a celebration. It's a reason to rejoice. And it's as simple and as complicated as that.

The Real Purpose of the Engagement

You're about to spend the next few months being feted because you found the right person to settle down with. You may have more than one party (engagement party, bachelorette party, wedding shower—to be discussed in more detail in Chapter 5) topped off by the one party to rule them all. You will swim in a pile of place cards, tulle, flowers . . . and spreadsheets and stress . . . while you plan your wedding. This can be, by turns, fun and overwhelming, but it is not the purpose of the engagement. The real reason for the engagement is to adjust to the idea of forming a brand-new family unit and making a major life transition. This period is about getting to know your fiancx's family in a different way and to allow you and your family of origin time to work through the inevitable changes.

Oh, and to fight.

The other reason for your engagement is to give you time to yell at each other, or to, um, gracefully hash out the big issues. It's better to yell your way through how you will set boundaries with your mother-in-law now than to fight your way through it the week following the wedding after suddenly realizing you don't see eye-to-eye on this *at all*.

Being engaged is not just about planning a wedding. Yes, you'll want to try on killer wedding outfits and make the perfect dance mix on Spotify. But this is also a time to focus on your relationship and discuss your shared dreams and goals.

ееее

Questions to Ask Before You Get Married

While I think everyone walking down the aisle should seek out premarital counseling (whether it's secular or religious in nature), it's also helpful to have tons of in-depth conversations

(continues)

with your partner in the comfort of your own home. With the help of the readers of APracticalWedding.com, I compiled this list of questions to kick off your discussions.

And while it's tempting to decide you're going to type-A the hell out of your relationship and answer all of these questions ASAP, be realistic about how much you can talk about and process at once. These are questions and conversations that will hopefully last a lifetime. And the answers to these questions will likely evolve over time for both of you, giving you reason to come back to the conversation again and again. But for now, pick a few areas that seem particularly important and start the conversation. While most questions are written in the first person, you should obviously both ask them of each other.

- **Faith**—What do you believe on a personal level? How do you view spirituality? Do you pray? What belief structure do we want in our household? What does that look like on a theoretical level? What does that look like day to day? What holidays will we celebrate and why?
- **Money**—What is the exact state of your finances? What are your assets and liabilities? How do you want to share finances? How do you feel about debt? What are your savings/financial goals? If one of us out-earns the other, how do we feel about that? How do we create equity, regardless of who earns what? What sort of life do we want to build together, and how much would that cost? Do either of us expect to support our parents at any point in our lives? What is the state of our parents' finances?
- **Goals**—What sort of careers do we want? How do we see family fitting into those careers? If one of us got a great job that required relocation, how would we feel about moving? Are we both willing to sacrifice equally for each other's dreams? How would we feel if one of our careers became significantly higher powered than the other? What expectations (stated or unstated) do we have about how each of our careers will progress and how we want to balance those careers? What sort of noncareer goals do we have? What is our vision for the life we want to create—beyond careers?

⸬ **Divorce**—What are your experiences with divorce? Would you agree to go to couple's counseling with me in a noncrisis situation if I requested it? Should we write a prenup?

⸬ **Kids/No Kids**—Do you want kids? How many? What if one of us changes our mind about kids? What if we are infertile? Are you open to adoption? Are you open to surrogacy or using donor sperm? What do we expect our parenting styles will be? How do we expect to share parenting duties? Are we planning on using child care so we both can continue to work? Does one of us want to be a stay-at-home parent? Would we want to get genetic screening before having a baby?

⸬ **Families**—What do we expect our relationships with our families of origin to look like? Does one or both of us have any conflicts with either family that we need to discuss? Do we feel like we're able to present a united front with our families? Do both of us feel supported by both families? How do we plan on handling disagreements with our families of origin? When our parents get ill, approach end of life, and die, how involved would we expect to be? How involved would we want our partner to be? Are there any family inheritance issues that need to be discussed?

⸬ **Location**—Do we want to live in an urban/suburban/rural environment? Are there locations that are a deal breaker for either of us? How do we feel about living near family?

⸬ **Fighting**—What's your argument style? What freaks you out when fighting? What is okay? How did your parents and loved ones fight, and how does that shape how you fight? Do you feel like our fighting style is healthy, or is it something we need to work on?

⸬ **Skeletons in the Closet**—Are there any difficult topics that you need to share? Were you physically or sexually abused at any point, or do you suspect that there might be childhood abuse that you don't remember? Did you experience any other significant traumas in childhood? Is there anything about past relationships that you need to bring up (emotional or physical abuse, STDs, unresolved emotional issues)? Is there a history of physical or mental illness for

(continues)

you or for your family? Is there anything I should know about you that I wouldn't know to ask?

⁊ **Sex**—How often do you expect to have it? Do you expect that to change over the years? Is there anything you like that I don't know about? Do we expect to be monogamous? Are either of us interested in an open relationship or in polyamory? What if one of us wanted to pursue this route, is that something we'd be open to discussing? What happens if one of us is unhappy with our sex life? Would we be willing to visit a sex therapist? What happens if one of us sleeps with someone once? What happens if one of us has a longer-term affair?

⁊ **Household Responsibilities**—How do we plan to divvy up chores and responsibilities? What happens if one of us isn't pulling our weight? Do we have similar standards for cleanliness and life organization? If not, are we willing to meet in the middle? If we had the resources to do so, would we be open to hiring help for household tasks? Does one of us feel like they're putting in significant amounts of emotional or invisible labor? Is there a way to work on balancing those responsibilities?

⁊ **Health**—Am I aware of any health issues that you have? Do you know that you are a carrier for any illnesses? Have you gotten DNA tests that reveal information about your health? Would you consider getting a DNA test to look at potential health issues? If one of us got sick, how would we expect to be cared for? Do you feel like you'd be up to the challenges of caring for me if I were seriously ill?

⁊ **End of Life**—What are our beliefs about death and/or the afterlife? What sort of end-of-life care does each of us expect? What do we each expect in terms of funeral and burial?

eeee

> We used our engagement as a boot camp to really address as many little bumps in our relationship as possible. We spent every week in premarital counseling during our engagement, which actually made the wedding day much more beautiful. Our vows had more meaning and depth than I could've ever imagined, and we both knew where we stood in ourselves and our marriage before we said "I do."
>
> —Aisha Allen, who married her partner at an elegant Queer San Francisco wedding

Brainstorming with Your Partner

So, you've relaxed. You've enjoyed being engaged. You've drunk a lot of celebratory champagne. Maybe you've even started having some long talks about what you want your marriage to be like. Now, you're ready to get started planning!

First, let me emphasize: this book is going to be about *two* people planning a wedding together. On your wedding day, there will be two people getting married. And while you might care more about color combinations than your partner does, they might end up caring more about the music than you do. And you won't know until you ask. So, it's time to sit down with your partner and have your first long wedding planning talk.

Step One: Crazy, Wild, Wonderful Dreams

The first thing to do is to brainstorm and to dream. Let yourself dream unrestricted by reality at first, because the heart has a way of guiding you in the right direction, even when the heart seems a little crazy. Ask yourself, if you could have any kind of wedding in the world, what would it be? Maybe you want to wear a silk shift dress as you get married under the Eiffel Tower after you've run away to live in Paris together. That's a pretty fantastic dream—write that down. What are your partner's crazy dreams? Write those down, too.

Once you've come up with your crazy dreams, think about why they make you grin. Maybe you are delighted by the idea of wearing a simple silk dress. Perhaps you really want a tiny wedding outside in a beautiful location. Or maybe it's as simple as wanting to feel like your wedding is the start of a great adventure. Write all of these ideas down. We're going to try to optimize the parts of the wedding that make you happy.

> My husband and I are atypical traditionalists. I know the indie-chic thing right now is the rustic wedding. But that's so not us. We wanted to channel Audrey Hepburn and Cary Grant at a lavish, jazz-music-pumpin', champagne-flowin', hot-damn party chock-full of garters and bouquet tosses and all the usual wedding junk. So we did. We got married on October 11 at 3 p.m. Yes, that's a Sunday. Yep, middle of the afternoon. We had a dessert reception.
>
> —Liz Moorhead, who married her husband in a hot-damn party in a church social hall

Step Two: Slightly More Pragmatic Details

Now that you've dreamed as crazy and as big as you can, use that information to figure out the type of wedding that you each think you want on a more pragmatic level. Don't worry if you don't agree at this point, but start by asking these questions:

≶ **Size**—What does each of you think is an ideal wedding size? Do you want a big party with all of your friends and family, or do you want a small ceremony at the courthouse? Ask yourself why. What is it about the wedding you have envisioned in your head that's important? Articulate this. Perhaps you want a big wedding because you have a big family, or maybe you just have a taste for glitz and figure this is one of the few chances you're going to have to throw a black-tie party. If you want a small wedding at the courthouse, maybe you don't like being the center of attention, or maybe you just want something as low-stress as possible. Write all of this down.

≶ **Vibe**—Ponder the kind of vibe you'd each like in your wedding. Jen Smith, who had a decidedly counterculture wedding in a hotel ballroom in Northern California, explained, "A wedding can be many things—fun, beautiful, religious, charming, traditional, exciting, quick, quirky, unusual, etc. Trying to plan a wedding that is *all* of those things would drive you insane pretty quickly. We decided that what we wanted was for the wedding to be fun and comfortable." You can't do it all, so figure out what's most important to you. Figure out what your vision is, as a duo. Maybe you want a crazy dance party or a small and elegant dinner party. Or maybe you want a laid-back picnic or a formal afternoon tea. Dreams that seem initially conflicting are okay, too. If you want a low-stress black-tie party, you're probably on to something. You're about to learn that the peculiar magic of weddings is that when you least expect it, they make the impossible possible.

≶ **That Lovin' Feeling**—Now, both you and your partner should ask yourselves: "What do I want our wedding to feel like?" Focus your ideal vibe on a feeling. A "champagne-flowin', hot-damn party" gives you a very specific sensation to shoot for—"pretty and purple" does not. Most of what you see in wedding magazines or websites focuses on how a wedding looks, so I want you to remember this (stick it on your fridge if you must): **"I will not remember what our wedding looked like; I will remember what it felt like."**

Step Three: Start Looking at Wedding Inspiration. Cautiously.

Once you've had these initial conversations, you're ready to start looking at wedding inspiration. As you start to move into the sometimes-frenzied inspiration phase of wedding planning, be wary. Starting a million wedding Pinterest boards and sweeping up all the wedding magazines at your local grocery store can start on a real high note, but can quickly become stressful if you try to figure out how to re-create all those amazing images. The truth is, the pictures you are looking at are not quite real. They've been edited to show you just the best and the prettiest moments of a wedding. They often have been created with a team of stylists and professionals. Trickier still, they are often created to look delightfully DIY and a little bit handmade—but the truth is that a whole lot of money was spent creating that look. So, enjoy the research, but make sure you step back from the edge. You are not keeping up with the Joneses of Pinterest. You likely don't have the time or the money. And once you realize the work that goes into it, you might not even have the desire. Focus on your very real wedding instead.

And the best way to do that can be to switch your focus from detail shots (as gorgeous as that lush bouquet is) to looking at people's real weddings. Now, of course, like everything else in wedding media, the real weddings you see are highly curated, and those photos are edited to show a very particular story. But even still, those real weddings can lead you to the thing that lights you up inside. What makes you feel tingly when you look at it? Perhaps it's a New Orleans wedding followed by a second line, where the stylish wedding party all wore matching white jumpsuits. Or maybe it's an Icelandic elopement for two and a fiery red ball gown rented online at the last minute. Perhaps it's the pot-luck wedding held in a church rec hall, where everyone looks overjoyed and there is pie instead of wedding cake. Or maybe it's the black-tie reception at one of the colleges at Oxford. Pay attention to that. Wedding pictures can allow you to break out of the box of What Is Always Done at Weddings and figure out what your heart desires. Maybe you see a bride in a slinky backless number, or in a feather cape, and you realize that, hey, a poufy white dress with conventional accessories is not for you. Brilliant! Write down or create a file of things that make you happy (or, yes, put it on a Pinterest board).

Step Four: The Wedding Mission Statement

Now you and your partner have a welter of ideas. Boil it down to a few key items. Maybe you want something affordable, low-stress, and fancy. That's great! I know those things sound conflicting, but it's still imma-nently possible.

. And as you do that, also think about your values. Is it important to you to have a religious ceremony? Are you doing this so you can gather your community together in one place? Do you have an amaz-ing, diverse community . . . that includes a bunch of less tolerant family members? If so, is creating inclusive safe space going to be key for you? What are the values that you want to include as you build this wedding from scratch?

Now use all of these ideas to create a simple sentence that I like to call "The Wedding Mission Statement." Once you've created the sen-tence that sums up what you're trying to do, and why you're trying to do it, put it on your fridge or somewhere you'll see it every day. Wedding planning sometimes takes on a life of its own, and you might suddenly find yourself crying while you call around trying to find a country club to fit your families' two-hundred-person guest list. When you can't figure out why you're so sad, you can come back to your stated goal of "small, relaxed, and fun wedding on the beach somewhere" and readjust.

"Part of our wedding planning was to come up with a possibility of what we wanted our wedding to be like. We chose Love, Ease, and Fun. If we got anxious about wedding choices, we would remind each other that if it wasn't love, ease, and fun, we didn't need to do it. It made planning so much less stressful. We used it as a mantra so much that when I started to feel stressed out and scared on the wedding day, a close friend said, "Love, ease, and fun, man. I'm not sure what it means, but it seems like you do." It returned the focus immediately to what the day was about. We've been married for over fifteen years now, and we still have people tell us that our wedding was the most loved-up, laid-back, fun party they have ever attended.

—Jay Pryor, a life coach who married their
wife in the Blue Ridge Mountains

Bringing in the Families

Families Are Complicated

As one of my friends told me at some stressed-out juncture or another during our planning, "There is a reason families don't go on the honeymoon." Oh boy, is that true. By which I mean to say, wedding planning can cause a lot more family stress than we imagine.

For most of our lives, we've absorbed messages from popular culture that weddings are a time to bond with our families and have wonderful, emotional, remember-on-our-deathbed moments with our mothers. The truth is, for most of us, families are loving, messy, complicated creatures. For many families, wedding planning looks nothing like it does in the movies. It involves a lot of hugs and smiles, but also a fair number of arguments and tears. This is normal.

In the modern world, since many couples live together before the wedding, the whole event is often mistaken for a purely symbolic rite of passage. But weddings are more than symbols—they change family dynamics in significant ways. During the wedding planning process, you are moving toward building a new primary family unit, and that can be stressful for everyone concerned. Understand that your wedding and your emerging family unit can be hard on your parents in ways that are difficult for you to grasp if you're not a parent yourself.

It's likely that what you are processing as a great joy, your parents may be processing as a loss. You're really grown now, and you're joining a new family unit. And just a second ago you were a baby. . . . And here come the waterworks. And since crying in front of everyone is terrible, they're just going to focus their many feelings on the seating chart. THE SEATING CHART, DAMN IT. Practice compassion and a real ability to listen.

Know What's Nonnegotiable

Because your wedding will likely be important and emotional for your families, it's valuable to know what's nonnegotiable for the two of you when you walk into the first conversation with your parents. Take that list of key ideas that you and your partner came up with and figure out what you can't budge on. Our list looked a little like this: a big-enough wedding so that we could invite all our closest friends and family, held in the area we were living, Jewish ceremony, and a kick-ass dance party. For us, those items were totally off the table for discussion, which meant when they came up in conversation with our parents, we *always* presented a united front. Remember that the choices that you are making about your wedding are the first choices you are making as a brand-new baby family, and they are practice for the much bigger choices that you have in front of you.

Then? Compromise, Compromise, Compromise

Once you've figured out your nonnegotiables and written your wedding mission statement, it's time to learn the key word for all weddings (heck, for everything that has to do with family, ever): *compromise*. Molly Wiedel Till, who got married on top of a mountain in Arizona and held her reception in a traditional social hall, explained how they approached balancing various interests: "For us, staying sane came down to just remembering what mattered to us—the ceremony and having a frickin' amazing dance party—and then remembering what mattered to the people we were spending this best day ever with—traditional stuff like open bars and garter tosses." Sit down with your families, ask what they care about, and really listen. Write it down. Then tell your families that you'll do your very best to balance everyone's needs and that you love them no matter what decisions you end up making.

The wedding day is not your day; it is everyone's day. But this is *your* wedding. So if your mom wants a three-hundred-person formal sit-down dinner at the Ritz, and you and your partner want a family-only ceremony at the courthouse, well, maybe you can have a formal sit-down dinner with your family after you go to the courthouse. Try to respect and honor your families' dreams for the wedding, but make sure that your emotional needs are being met first and foremost.

ℯℯℯℯ

The Unique Challenges of Planning a Queer Wedding

By Jamie Thrower of Studio XIII Photography

I started my career as a wedding photographer seven years ago. I photograph the LGBTQ community almost exclusively, because the wedding industry can be a specifically challenging (and, let's just call it what it is, awkward) place for Queer folks. I listened a lot to the experiences of my clients and friends who were getting married and had a good idea of how navigating the wedding world can create a unique set of challenges for the LGBTQ community. But it wasn't until I got engaged myself last fall that I really had firsthand experience of how strange and alienating it can be.

Since then, I've found myself staring down inquiry forms with "bride and groom" as the only places to fill in information. I've struggled to find an outfit that makes my curvy, femme self feel seen. My fiancx and I are more likely to be assumed sisters or friends than partners. And because we don't play into any stereotypical gender roles, most wedding traditions feel strange to us.

The LGBTQ community has been able to legally marry in the United States since 2015, but there are still so many obstacles to planning and having a wedding. Here are some of the most challenging things that have come up for me, my friends, and my clients while planning a wedding as a Queer person.

Money. Money. Money.

As a community, many LGBTQ-identified folks lack the resources or funds to cover the high price of weddings. Many of us are paying for the wedding ourselves due to lack of "traditional" family support, which makes budgeting or even thinking about the price of a wedding seem impossible. Add to that the fact that LGBTQ people face a disproportionate amount of discrimination and barriers to employment, and you often have a situation where money is tight. (Or tighter than it is for many of our straight/cis peers.)

While there might not be a way to increase your budget feasibly, the Queer community is rooted in being creative and thinking outside the box. The first step? Find a budget that works for you and prioritize what is most important to have at your wedding. Have a skill? I've found that some vendors accept trade or partial trade for services to cut down costs, while others may be open to creating a payment plan for you, instead of having to cough up a big chunk all at once. But beyond vendors, this is the time to ask your community for help. While they may not be able to financially contribute, friends and family want to be a part of your wedding—whether that's

(continues)

baking pies instead of an expensive cake or helping make decorations, calling on your community to help bring together
your wedding vision can be really rewarding and make your
wedding even more special.

Finding That Killer Outfit

I'm a cisgender Queer femme and I've always imagined myself wearing a dress at my wedding. This makes walking into a
wedding shop easier for me. But for gender nonconforming,
trans, nonbinary, or folks who want to wear something other
than what is deemed "traditional" for their gender presenta-
tion, finding a wedding outfit can feel like an impossible task.
I'm so glad that there are more suiting companies that are
dedicated to tailoring for Queer bodies, and this is a huge step
in the right direction. But we need more of them, as well as
femme clothes for non-cisgender female bodies. Anyone who
is getting married should be able to walk into a store and buy
a kick-ass wedding outfit, while not being immediately labeled
as a bride or a groom.

Looking beyond "Bridal/Wedding" stores for clothes can
be very helpful. Check vintage shops, Etsy, or other stores
that carry unique pieces of clothing that will feel more like
you. Or hey, commission someone to make something custom
that will be 100 percent unique and true to you!

Heteronormativity and Lack of Diversity

The constant bombardment of "bride and groom" and "Mr.
and Mrs." is everywhere, and most companies who are involved in the wedding industry are marketing toward "brides
and grooms." It shows in their advertising, the copy they use
on their websites, the photos that they show, and the intake
forms on their contact pages. My fiancx and I are usually
able to laugh it off, but we also recognize that it's annoying
to have to cross out or asterisk when it says "groom's info"
because neither one of us identifies as a groom. Even in the
LGBTQ wedding world, we see most weddings described as
"same-sex weddings," which doesn't leave room for the nu-
ances and identities of those in Queer relationships.

When looking for vendors for your wedding, seek out
businesses who are inclusive of all Queer relationships—you

can do this by searching terms or hashtags like "Queer wedding" or "LGBTQ wedding" instead of "same-sex wedding." There are also lists compiled each year of LGBTQ-friendly wedding vendors/businesses that are a great resource for finding someone in your area. Sometimes, though, you might not be able to find or use the person/business that you love, so if you have the capacity, make a note to vendors who might have only heteronormative forms that they might want to update their copy/contracts to be more inclusive. (This is how we bring about change, right?)

Outdated Gender Roles and Stereotypes

I work with a lot of genderqueer, nonbinary, and trans folks who feel erased from the wedding industry altogether. While there's some great "Gay Wedding" stuff out there, a lot of it is stereotypical, or exclusive of other Queer identities. I remember being at a wedding where the venue put out a sign that said "two brides are better than one," which, while well intended, was awkward for the couple with one person in a suit not identifying as a bride at all. Society gets stuck in gender roles and assumes anyone who is masculine/feminine presenting should fall into the correlating gender role, and vice versa. There are also many vendors and industry folks that don't know to (or care to) ask pronouns and end up misgendering their couples on their wedding day.

Stating your pronouns right off the bat to vendors (and asking theirs) can set the example for them and hopefully make things less awkward down the road. I've also found that having an advocate on your wedding day (and throughout the wedding planning process) has been really helpful for folks, especially regarding pronouns or outdated stereotypes. This person can also help you not feel pressured into participating in any gendered or outdated "wedding traditions" that you don't want to do.

The (Very Real) Fear of Discrimination

One of the biggest fears that I've heard from couples is that they'll be discriminated against by vendors. And while I like to

(continues)

think that most people in the wedding industry wouldn't deny someone based on who they love, it happens *all the time*. It breaks my heart to hear these stories, or to hear the fears and firsthand experiences of my clients and friends.

While the fear and reality of discrimination are very prevalent, I know from experience that there are some really amazing Queer-identified or LGBTQ-friendly folks in the industry. There are lists compiled every year to help couples take the guesswork out of it, so you can trust that when you reach out, you'll be treated with respect, dignity . . . and, most likely, excitement! (A Practical Wedding and Equally Wed both offer online vendor directories that are great resources.) Once you find Queer-friendly vendors, they can often serve as references for other vendors in your area who provide excellent service to the LGBTQ community.

Family Can Be a Sore Subject

Family support often looks different for Queer folks, and it can be painful to explain to someone why your father won't be walking you down the aisle or why family members weren't invited to the wedding. I've showed up to shoot a wedding and been the only witness. I've had couples who have told me that their family won't be attending because they don't agree with "LGBTQ marriage." I've seen family members misgender people in speeches.

Being honest and open about the feelings that arise from these complicated family dynamics can be healing. That might mean having conversations with your partner, with a therapist, or with friends, or just letting yourself feel your feelings. Your wedding is about you and your partner, so feel free to leave problematic or painful family members off the invite list and, instead, surround yourself with the people whom you love and who love you back. Queers have always been defining their families for themselves, and that's what makes the community so special and resilient.

Queer folks are getting married—and we're doing it our way, on our terms, with our unique identities and resilience in tow. Finding the right vendors and people to participate in, support, and be a part of our weddings is tough, but it's not gonna stop us from defying the norms while celebrating and

affirming our love. Because that's what Queerness is, and always has been.

ℓℓℓℓ

The Anti To-Do List

Now you've talked with your partner, and you've talked to your families. At this point the two of you should have a pretty clear idea of what you'd like to aim for, if reality doesn't get in the way. Before we get into the nitty-gritty of planning, it's time to take a moment to think of what you don't need to do (because there is so, so much of it).

Print out one of those endless wedding checklists from the Internet or find one in a magazine. Sit down with a friend who has already gotten married (and has a good head on their shoulders) and a cocktail. Get out a red pen, and circle only the things that are absolutely necessary. By necessary, I mean you should have a list that reads something like this:

- a partner whom you love (if this wasn't listed on your preprinted list, feel free to write it in nice and big at the top)
- an officiant
- witnesses
- something to wear

Then take a blue pen and circle the things that you actually care about. Not the stuff that your Wedding Self cares about, or the stuff you think you Have to Care About, or the stuff the list tells you that you Have to Care About, but the stuff *you* actually care about. Then, next to each item, write *why* you care or *how* you care. Maybe you care about invitations because you majored in studio art in college. Maybe you care about what you're going to eat because you are really passionate about food. Maybe you hate wedding cake, but you really want to cut a wedding blackberry cobbler. Great! Write those things down.

Then take a pen and cross out every single other thing.

It's not that you can't do any of the things that you crossed out; it's that now you have given yourself permission to not care about them. Chairs? Yes, you probably need them. But unless they made it onto your blue-pen list, you have magically been freed from worrying about chair covers, or memorizing the different kinds of chairs you can rent in increasing order of price (folding, banquet, bent wood, Chiavari). Why? Because it does not really matter to you. And when all is said and done? It really won't matter.

Remember What You Care About

In this chapter, I made you write down more than a few things: the list of your crazy, wild dreams, the vibe of the party you want, and your tentative wedding plan. I asked you to find out what your families care about and write that down. Plus, I made you work through that long wedding magazine list, circling the stuff that made you happy and crossing off all the stuff you didn't care about. Here is the key step: keep these lists. Pin the lists to your fridge or put them somewhere you can easily find. We're about to dive into the nitty-gritty parts of wedding planning, and sometimes what you really want has a way of getting lost under what you think you have to have. And you're going to need some touchstones of sanity during this process.

WEDDING HOMEWORK

○ Enjoy *just being engaged* before you do a single thing. Type A's in the house, I see you right now. Stop trying to make everything happen at once, and go throw some confetti, or cuddle on the couch, or pop some bubbly. The moment of being freshly engaged will not pass this way again, so enjoy it before you do anything else on this list.

○ Think about what you want to create with this wedding. What are your wedding values? What images delight you? Do you want to create community, have a really fun party, celebrate religious ritual, or all of the above? Discuss this (maybe over a celebratory drink) and come up with a simple wedding mission statement that you can come back to when things get confusing. It might look something like this: "We want a laid-back dance party that celebrates our community and feels really fun." Whatever it is, make sure it's a clear and simple vision that will steer your choices.

○ Figure out what your wedding nonnegotiables are. Write them down.

○ If you have a good relationship with your families of origin (or you have amazing chosen families) sit down with them and ask about what they care about . . . and really listen. See if you can fold those wants and needs into your wedding plan. Because while it might be your wedding, it's everyone-who-loves-you's day.

○ Seek out premarital counseling if you can. If you don't have the ability to work with a professional, set up a few times to sit down and go through the questions on pages 6–8. This isn't just about planning a wedding; it's about planning a life together.

○ Find a good, long wedding checklist somewhere and then sit down and circle everything that's actually necessary. Then take a different color pen and circle everything you or your partner really, truly, deep down cares about. Then cross off every other thing on that damn list and put it on your fridge.

○ Write this mantra everywhere and say it in the mirror every morning: "I will not remember what our wedding looked like; I will remember what it felt like."

{ 2 }

The Basics: Who, Where, When, How

 Beyond the Spreadsheets

⸭ Throw out the tried-and-true wedding template you have in your head and start thinking big. Once you start thinking outside the box, you'll realize that anyone, in any circumstance, with any amount of money, can make a wedding happen.

⸭ Formulating your guest list can be a complex dance of balancing the needs of many people, not to mention dealing with logistics. (Sorry about that in advance.) But when all is said and done, remember that the people you need are the ones who show up.

⸭ If the venue search feels overwhelming, you're not alone. But no matter how much you'd like to do, well, *anything* else, it's important to pick your venue before you jump into planning the rest of your wedding. The time and place set the tone for the wedding, and the last thing you need is to purchase a wedding dress that doesn't work for the location and season.

(continues)

- When looking at traditional venues, make sure you understand all the costs and fees and ask lots of questions.
- Look for unexpected options. Many big cities have affordable public wedding venues in parks, or you can rent a picnic spot or overlook point. Neighborhood restaurants, bars, cafés, even chain restaurants with event spaces can offer tasty food and affordable style. Plus, don't ignore those old-school social halls.
- If you want a small wedding, look at having an at-home or courthouse wedding, or eloping.
- If you need to make this whole project a little less expensive, think about having your wedding at a less popular time—during the day, midweek, or in the winter.
- You don't need to serve a full meal during your reception, but if you do, remember you can consider less traditional options for food service.
- Stop trying to force your wedding into the box of How Everyone Else Is Doing It, and just let it be what it is. It's going to be excellent.

The Magic of Weddings (Anywhere Works)

The Internet has endlessly expanded the wedding ideas available to us, all while increasing the pressure to come up with a perfectly "us" wedding. But that endless wedding personalization still tends to exist within a limited, and often binary, framework. The gospel of wedding media tells you that you can have one of two things—the full shebang (ceremony, followed by seated meal, followed by wild dance party), or you can ditch it all and elope. But the real secret is that your wedding can look however you need it to look. So if you've been spending hours and hours trying to figure out how to make a specific kind of wedding work for you, even if deep down you're not sure you want it, feel free to stop. Because there are so, so many options: practical options, simple options, affordable options, and—best—subvert-the-paradigm options (because yes, you can totally make that hotel wedding exactly what you need it to be).

In this chapter, we'll discuss the fundamental building blocks of a wedding—the who, where, when, and how. First, we'll look at your guest list, and then we'll walk through the wedding venue search and discuss the delights of morning and off-season weddings. Finally, we'll discuss the central question of planning a wedding reception: "How are we going to feed these people?" Historically, weddings were a ceremony and then some sort of celebration. And when you simplify it to that level, you have a world of choices.

~~~~

My Husband Planned Our Whole Wedding

By Megan Kongaika

I'll be honest. I began planning my wedding before I was even out of the womb. From the dress, to the walk down the aisle with my dad, to the entire town of guests, to my first dance, to the party favors—it was all orchestrated (in my head) like a MasterCard commercial. But then things changed.

Paul proposed two weeks before Christmas. Two months later, my father lost his yearlong battle to cancer. This devastating event left us all exhausted and grieving. I'd looked forward to planning a wedding all of my life, but following my father's death it felt difficult and awkward to even attempt to muster excitement about doing so. I also didn't want to put off the wedding, as Paul had seen me through the most difficult year of my life, and I was ready to officially begin our journey together.

So, with the exception of four contributions, Paul planned our wedding.

My husband and I are very different. He's a Pacific Islander (born and raised in Tonga) and fully embodies the spirit of the island. "Laid-back" doesn't even begin to describe it. In

(continues)

contrast, I'm a Montana girl who would prefer to plan my own surprise birthday party. By that I mean I would lead guests in the birthday song if no one appeared to be making it happen. He prefers to simply let things play out—to "see how it goes." I lean toward a more commandant approach.

Given that information, it came as a surprise to some (hi, Mom!) that I was willing to give up control and hand the reins over to Paul. Sure, I fought back a grand mal seizure when my husband said we didn't need to have a guest list, but it got easier.

Other than buying two plane tickets to Hawaii (contribution #1), inviting our closest friends and family (contribution #2), buying a $150 dress online (contribution #3), and saying a Hail Mary that, at the end of the day, Paul and I would end up married (contribution #4), I pretty much left it up to him.

On the morning of our wedding, I was fairly quiet on the way to the church as I pondered how this whole thing might come together. With the exception of my few contributions, I'd put the entire day in the hands of Paul and his very traditional Tongan family. Secretly, I wondered and worried if I'd be able to hide any disappointment I thought I was bound to feel by not having things go exactly as I'd always imagined. I'd confessed this concern to my mother the day before. She calmly grabbed my shoulders and whispered, "It will be glorious. It will be just as it should be." She trusted him. I decided to follow suit.

When I walked into the church, I fought back tears as I took in the entire scene. There were flowers, and bows, and music piping through the church sound system. Traditional Tongan tapa cloths lined the floor like royal rugs. The reception area was completely set up, and more than forty of my fiancé's relatives were there to greet us warmly with welcoming smiles.

Before I knew it, Paul and I were decked out in traditional Tongan wedding gear. I met our ring bearer (surprise!) seconds before we walked down the aisle. I met our vocalist (surprise!). Then the music started, and it was showtime.

As my stepdad of twenty-five years walked me down the aisle, I thought to myself, "Paul pulled it off. He really did it." My closest friends and family were surrounding me, the man of my dreams who'd made it all happen was waiting for me at the end of the aisle, and everything was just as it was supposed to have been. Paul and his family had given me the most wonderful wedding I could have ever imagined. *This* was the moment that mattered.

When people ask me about my wedding day, I tell them that despite being unable to take credit for nearly all of it, there isn't one thing that I would have changed.

So, thank you to my husband, Paul, for planning our wedding. It was nothing like I'd pictured it would be all of my life. It was better.

ℓℓℓℓ

Who: The Guest List—How Hard Can It Be?

Let's start at the beginning. Before you do anything else (like, say, pick a venue), you need to have a rough idea of how many people you plan to invite. My suggestion is that you start the conversation by asking, "Whom do we love? Who *must* be there?" And then work backward till you have a number. The trick is to figure out how many people you want around you on your wedding day, and then figure out how you can afford to celebrate with them. There is nothing wrong with getting the two hundred people you love most in the world together and feeding them cake and punch on a Sunday afternoon in the park. Do not listen to anyone who tells you that you must cut your guest list to afford a wedding. The most important thing is to gather the people who love you. Once you do that, the details will iron themselves out.

As you're working, keep in mind that for many couples, the seemingly simple project of figuring out whom to invite, and then inviting them, is one of the most fraught parts of planning. Guest lists are the single biggest outward manifestation of the power struggles that accompany a wedding. (Who gets to invite whom? What sort of a wedding is this anyway? What do you mean I can't invite whomever I want?) In addition, guest lists tend to expose the rift between how you wish things were and reality. You love so-and-so, but you haven't seen her in years. You were so sure so-and-so was going to come, but then he bowed out. Unfortunately, there is no magic solution for this other than crying it out and discussing it. The best I can tell you is that, when all is said and done, the people who show up to support you on your wedding day will be the important ones.

Tips for Creating Your Guest List with Minimal Tears

Building a guest list can be tricky. Before you start developing the list, here are some issues to think through:

- **Who is paying?** If your parents are helping to pay for the wedding, it's reasonable to expect that they will want to invite people they care about (in fact, it's reasonable to expect this even if they are not paying). That said, when accepting the money, it's fair for you to set some limits on what that guest list will look like because, no matter what, you want to get married surrounded by people who know you and love you.

- **Knowing you versus knowing of you.** Your parents have their own social life. They have friends from work who don't know you at all, and they have old friends whom you haven't seen since you were a toddler. It can be helpful to give your parents general guidelines about whom you feel comfortable having at your wedding, but also make exceptions. Sometimes your parents do know best, and the most fun wedding guest will be the one you haven't seen since you were three.

- **Are you still close?** It can be tempting to want to invite everyone who's invited you to his or her wedding, or old friends from high school that you haven't seen in ages. But that isn't mandatory.

When shaping the guest list, think about whom you are close to currently, not just whom you wish you were still in touch with.

➤ **Are you inviting plus-ones?** In recent years, it's become fairly standard to extend a plus-one to single wedding guests. And while it's not mandatory (unless we're talking about your friend's long-term partner, and then it absolutely is), it is kind. Showing up to a wedding by yourself when everyone else is coupled up is daunting—and makes it likely that those guests will RSVP no. But if you're not choosing to (or able to) offer folks the ability to bring a date—for goodness' sake, sit them next to someone fun.

➤ **Are you inviting kids?** You can invite kids, or not invite kids. But it's best to keep the rule consistent (though babes in arms and children in the wedding party should always get an invite). (For far more depth on keeping your parent friends happy with your kid-free wedding, see below.)

Remember that answering these questions is just the beginning of the puzzle—and diplomatic-level negotiation—that often comprises finalizing the wedding guest list. Whether you're trying to limit your courthouse elopement to twenty people or negotiating your Orthodox Jewish family down to a guest list of four hundred from their dream guest list of six hundred, difficult decisions are going to have to be made, and people are going to have to be told no. Which is all as it should be—and very good practice for the life ahead of you.

ℓℓℓℓ

How to Have a Child-Free Wedding

Kids can be a joy at your wedding, and weddings can be a great way to celebrate with a multigenerational community. That

(continues)

said, there are times when it just doesn't work to have tiny humans at your wedding.

The first question worth asking yourselves honestly (the honest answer is not to be repeated outside the four walls of your home) is this: Do we care if the parents on our guest list attend? It's possible the answer is no. If that's the case, take care of step one, below, and then move on. But let's assume you do really hope the parents on your guest list come. What follows are the best possible tricks for getting your parent friends in the door, kid-free.

Let Everyone Know Early

The time to let people know that your wedding is going to be adults only is when you send out your save the dates. Yes, technically, if kids are not included in an address on the save the date or invitation, they're not invited, but on this one you need to have a more obvious approach. If you have just a few parent friends, go for one-on-one communication. However, if this isn't practical, a wedding website is a great place for conveying this information thoughtfully. Remember, your job is to communicate your needs and expectations around the wedding as clearly and kindly as possible. Once you do that, people will make their own choices.

Traveling, Child Care, and Other Things to Think About

If most of your guests are local, having an adults-only wedding is going to be relatively straightforward for most parents in the crowd. However, if people are going to be traveling in from out of town, that likely means they need to find child care in an unfamiliar city. To maximize parental attendance, it's helpful to come up with a list of trusted child-care providers who can come to the hotel, campsite, church, or wherever the wedding is being held. Provide this list (or let people know you will be providing this list) as early as possible. The extra-credit option is to offer on-site child care. If you have the budget and space and know that you have a number of parents who will use it, it's a great way to keep the ceremony and reception child-free, while still making kids feel included.

Babes in Arms

If you have any new (and possibly nursing) parents in the crowd, consider bending the no-kid rule for them. New parenthood is isolating, and if you can avoid your girlfriend's having to sit out a wedding because the baby won't take a bottle, do it. Don't worry about other parents being upset. "She's nursing, and it's the only way she could come" is explanation enough.

ՓՓՓՓ

RSVP Rates

The final puzzle of wedding guest lists is figuring out just how many people you can invite, given the space you have. And while it's tempting to imagine that because everyone loves you so much, they'll all show up . . . that's likely not what will happen. They do, of course, love you a ton. But love doesn't mitigate the realities of distance, expense, vacation leave, health, scheduling, and any other number of issues.

When putting together your guest list, you're stuck guessing how many people you should invite to fill the amount of space you have. So, notwithstanding cataclysmic events (our wedding invitations went out shortly after the economy had very nearly collapsed, drastically reducing the number of people who could afford to travel to our wedding), here are the rough numbers you need in order to calculate what your RSVP rates might be:

- **Average total RSVP rate:** 75 percent attendance
- **Local guests:** 85–90 percent attendance
- **Nonlocal guests:** 65–75 percent attendance (depending on holidays, ease of travel, and appeal of the location)
- **Family:** 85 percent
- **Friends:** 50 percent
- **Weddings under fifty guests:** 90 percent

The People You Need Are the Ones That Show Up

In the depth of wedding planning, having faith that you are making the right choices with your guest list can be hard. We had some painful moments: close friends who canceled on the wedding with little reason, loved ones who couldn't come due to financial constraints, confusion over whom we should invite. In the end, I wish I'd known how it would feel. When you walk down the aisle, the people who are there are the ones that matter—those people, and the people you hold in your heart.

Where: The Quest for a Wedding Venue

Now that you have an idea of what kind of wedding you and your partner want, your families' thoughts on the subject, and at least a vague guess as to how many people you plan on inviting, it's time to look for a wedding venue. Please heed me when I tell you that you should look for a wedding venue *before you do anything else* (other than discuss your budget; see Chapter 3 for more on that). I'm not generally one for hard-and-fast rules, but in this case it's practical. Looking for a wedding venue can be a real pain, and it's tempting to want to skip that step for a while and move on to the fun things, like dress shopping. The thing is, where and when you hold your wedding (the location, the time of day, the season) will dictate most of the rest of your planning. You don't want to run off and buy a dress you love, only to find that your indie-eloping-in-Vegas sheath doesn't work at all at the garden-in-the-middle-of-a-forest wedding you end up throwing.

While picking a venue can feel immense, it's not a life-or-death decision. Catherine Sly, who married in a simple civil service before holding her reception in a hotel function room in Brighton, England, told me, "We only looked at one reception venue. People asked me if I didn't feel like I should look around more, but I just thought, 'We're having a party there, not buying the place.'" So stop stressing out, and get cracking. Once you've picked the venue, it will feel as if a huge weight has lifted off your shoulders and like this wedding thing is for real.

The Traditional Wedding Venue

A logical place to start the search is often in online wedding venue directories. This will tend to limit your search to the classic wedding venue, for better or worse. Venues that cater specifically to weddings tend to be relatively more expensive and sometimes require longer lead times than nontraditional venues. They do, however, have their strengths. If you don't want to have to cart away your own trash at the end of the night or supply your own tables, a traditional venue is the way to go.

Keep in mind that if you really want to make it easy on yourself, you can look for an all-inclusive wedding venue—what one might call a party factory. They exist in most major cities (though not in the super-hip parts of town) and in pretty much every resort in any tropical destination you can think of. They might host several weddings, b'nai mitzvot, quinceañeras, retirement parties, or more in a day. These parties don't reinvent the wheel. You'll usually rely on the same florist, baker, caterer, and photographer that everyone else does. But due to economy of scale (that photographer is going to shoot up to three weddings on one day alone), it keeps costs down, while still letting you have all of the bells and whistles. Plus, with a staff that knows exactly what they are doing, and without a thousand personalized decisions to make, an all-inclusive venue can really reduce stress. Lisa Dennis said, "To keep my sanity, it was worth it to us to pay the price to have our reception at a place that would cover all the food, the setup, and the cleanup. Worrying about that could've killed me." Know your limitations. If you want a full-service venue, then by all means, your sanity is worth it.

However, it's important to walk into a wedding venue prepared to ask the right questions. Because, trust me, nothing is quite so fun as finding out you just paid $5,000 for a totally empty room with no staff.

Things to Think About When Looking at Traditional Wedding Venues

⇝ **Are tables and chairs provided?** Do not assume that they are, and do not assume that renting them will be cheap. Find out exactly what is provided and who sets up and tears down.

⇝ **What is the staff situation?** What staff members are included in your flat fee, and what will they take care of? Are there additional staff members that they suggest (or require) you to hire? Should you expect to tip staff?

⇝ **Can you bring your own alcohol?** There are few things that will save you more money than being able to provide your own wine and beer. Instead of paying $12 a cocktail (ouch!), you can pay $12 for a whole bottle of wine. So! Do your research. Paying a little more for a venue that will let you bring the booze will often save you lots of money in the final calculation.

⇝ **Are you locked into a catering contract?** Many venues either require that you use an on-site caterer or provide you with a list of preferred caterers. This can sometimes be more expensive, so it's good to know about up front and then price that into the cost of the venue. All-inclusive venues often use in-house caterers, which will be part of your final bill. (They don't tend to offer much in the way of creativity, but they will keep your costs down.)

⇝ **Additional fees.** Is there a cake-cutting fee? A corkage fee? A cleanup fee? Added fees are standard industry practice. Ask questions about additional fees before you sign a contract (and for more on contracts, please do yourself a favor and see Chapter 5).

Other Places to Throw a Fabulous Party (That Happens to Celebrate Your Marriage)

Maybe you want to get a little adventurous. Maybe you want to save money, or maybe you just want to color outside the wedding lines. You've decided that a traditional wedding venue is not for you and want to explore other options.

Weddings, as presented by the wedding industry, are parties with a very strict formula: ceremony, cocktails and appetizers, sit-down dinner, cake cutting, first dance, dance party, send-off. We'll discuss in Chapter 4 how none of this is particularly traditional—but when everyone tells you it's the Way Things Are Done, it's easy to start feeling trapped. We start thinking that we need a ceremony site, a place to have cocktails, and a dance floor. But the truth is, weddings don't need any of these prescribed elements.

Stop thinking about throwing a wedding and start thinking about throwing a party. What kind of parties do you normally throw or attend? Do your tastes run to dinner parties? Picnics? Gatherings in religious social halls? Bashes in the middle of the desert? All-night dance parties? Excellent. Now start considering the size of your wedding and how you would throw those parties if you needed to make them a little bigger. Where would you throw a nonwedding party? What would the location be? Now you're talking.

Parks: Trade Your Wedding Planner for a Park Ranger

We got married in a wedding venue located on an enormous piece of local parkland, and we could not have made a better choice. The key advantages were price, stunning scenery, not having to deal with wedding people (just park rangers), and the fact that every penny we paid went to supporting our local parks. Of course, parks have their drawbacks. As government-owned entities, there are often very strict regulations and time limits that you must adhere to. That felt like a fair compromise to us, but in reality we didn't think about the regulations for a hot second on our wedding day (and the four-year-olds still ended up sneaking off to play in the flower beds, allowed or not).

You'd be surprised at the number of traditional wedding venues located in parks. But beyond that, another underutilized venue is the modern picnic site. You can fancy-up a picnic site with white tablecloths and candles, bring in food from a local restaurant, and have an elegant outdoor dinner party wedding. Or put down colorful blankets, rent a taco truck, and have a hip picnic wedding. Keep in mind, though, when you throw your wedding at a nontraditional venue, you'll be responsible for setup, cleanup, and often trash disposal. Decide if you're up for dish washing and trash hauling (and the associated costs) before you get too sucked into the really romantic parts of your wedding under the stars. With a picnic space, you have an affordable blank canvas to do almost anything (but that anything is going to include picking up after yourself as well).

And, finally, consider saying your vows in a park and having the celebration elsewhere. Many national and state parks have beautiful overlook points, gazebos, or spots by a lake where you can have your friends and loved ones gather while you say your vows, and then you can dash off to a local restaurant or backyard to celebrate.

Restaurants: Just Look Around Your Neighborhood

While it's perfectly possible to have a really expensive wedding in a really fancy restaurant, there are also tons of smaller neighborhood restaurants that are delighted to host weddings, affordably. Start looking at restaurants you like to go to regularly, along with cafés, and, yes, even bars. Consider that Mexican place with the big back room; look at the brunch place you like to go on Sunday mornings; check out the pub with the exposed brick walls. Heck, look into the big chain restaurant with the back room that does balloon bouquets for birthday parties—who's to say you couldn't make some seriously unexpected wedding magic happen there (with a balloon garland)? The best part is finding out how thrilled many of these businesses are to host a wedding. Plus, they have the additional bonus of being pros at serving a meal . . . and cleaning up after one. No dish washing for you!

Cara Winter, who held her reception at a farm-to-table restaurant in Brooklyn, explained the advantages of a restaurant wedding this way: "If you're considering a completely DIY decorated party in the parish hall, consider this: if just explaining the aesthetic to your mom leads to a stress-induced meltdown, and you've never actually made anything by hand before, you might want to evaluate whether the extra couple thousand to do it at a chic no-decorations-needed restaurant is worth it. My sanity was worth about $1,850." Restaurants are brilliant, not just because the food is bound to be good, but also because they come predecorated and prestaffed. You just show up and have a party.

Social Halls: Spinning Straw into Gold

We have all gotten so indoctrinated with the idea that weddings happen in beautiful wedding *venues*, that it seems a bit of a throwback to consider having your reception (and even your ceremony) in a social hall. But it is always worthwhile to look around you to see what social halls you have at your disposal—from halls at your local place of worship, to veterans' halls, to old-school social clubs—and then figure out if you can use a little joy and style to make the place glorious. Morgan Turigan, who married in Calgary, Canada, did just that: "We had a cheapish wedding. It was not full of charming details or at a beautiful venue or full of indie spirit. It was at a plain hall with minimal decoration, and it was so full of love and family that I couldn't stop beaming." In the end, it's not the beauty of the wedding venue that makes the party; it's your joy and the joy of the people who have gathered around you. If the way you can afford to get everyone you love in one place is by hosting your reception at a public social hall, do it. Yes, some of these places are less than beautiful, but you'd be surprised what some flowers and joy can do to a place.

And Anywhere Else You Can Imagine

You can throw a wedding just about anywhere if you're willing to think outside the box. I've heard of weddings held at summer camps, youth hostels, rented vacation homes, apple orchards, and public beaches. However, the further outside the box you go, the more you need to think about practicalities like hiking boots, porta potties, and trash disposal. The list is only limited by your imagination and your moxie, so get dreaming.

The Simplest Weddings

When we look at the history of weddings in the United States (which we will do in more depth in Chapter 4), we see a long tradition of simple weddings. For hundreds of years, weddings in this country took place in people's homes. During World War II, a huge number of weddings took place at the courthouse with the bride in her best clothes, always wearing flowers. We've lost track of these simple traditions in a flurry of ever bigger and more complicated weddings. But there is something profoundly beautiful about these simple celebrations. They can be done quickly and easily, allowing the focus to be on the love between two people.

At-Home Weddings and Backyard Weddings

Weddings are (or should be) a slightly more dignified version of the parties that you already throw, so if you or your parents have a home you feel comfortable entertaining in, you have a home that is perfect for a small wedding. Author Emma Straub, who had a simple wedding in Manhattan, told me, "We ended up with about thirty people in my parents' dining room. I wore my mother's dress and a piece of tulle the size of a pumpkin on my head. It was packed and warm and perfect—I was surrounded by people I love. What could be better?" And that's the magic of the at-home wedding. It's not fussy, but having the people you love in a place you call home is its own kind of wonderful.

When preparing your home for a wedding, I'd suggest that you hire a housekeeper to make the place spotless possibly before, and definitely after, the wedding, and maybe hire someone to serve and clean up the food. Podcaster Kathleen Shannon, who got married in her 1920s bungalow in Oklahoma City, said, "Trust me, there was nothing romantic about mopping down our wood floors, sticky with spilled liquor, the morning after our wedding." But beyond making sure your house is clean and you have something to wear, there is not a whole lot that you *must* do for an at-home wedding, which is incredibly liberating.

You'll need a place to say your vows and a place for your guests to sit (which may mean procuring extra chairs, by either renting them or borrowing them). You'll need a table on which to spread food and some space for mingling, or a setup for a small dinner party or luncheon. Homes and backyards offer you a chance to create your wedding from scratch—to decorate as little or as much as you want; to make your own food or have it catered from a local restaurant; to have a dance party on the back patio; to have a formal dinner party in the living room. And in the end, what you'll be left with are the best memories in the world, every time you walk through the door.

The Courthouse Wedding

When I first wrote this book, courthouse weddings were still something of a rare event. These days at my job, we see photos of as many city hall weddings as we do traditional weddings. And it's no puzzle as to why. Many city halls are beautiful buildings that you can use for free. Plus, eloping at the courthouse gives you the perfect excuse to ditch anything you don't care about. Get a cute outfit, some flowers, and the people you care about the most (and maybe a photographer to document that cute outfit), and you can head off to get married at a moment's notice. It's easy to get caught up in thinking that you need to make your wedding day complicated and stressful to make it feel special. But your wedding day will be important no matter what because it's the day you vow to spend your life with another person. Lindsay Whitfield, who had a simple wedding at the courthouse while eight months pregnant, said, "I was worried that without an audience made up of family and friends, I wouldn't recognize the solemnity of the moment. But the second I walked down the aisle, saw my husband, and realized what we were about to do, the solemnity and sacredness of the moment overwhelmed me." Courthouse weddings narrow the focus to a ritual that moves couples to the other side—a ritual that makes them a family.

> We talked a lot about the "minimum viable wedding," which for us was a few of our favorite humans, a cool location, rad outfits, and an insanely good photographer. Once we had all of that stuff, we came up with some fun projects to make our wedding feel more like "us," as bonus extra-awesomeness. Since we thought of all that stuff as extra, we weren't stressed about it at all!
>
> —Maggie Winters Gaudaen, cofounder of tiny pop-up wedding company Pop! Wed Co., married her partner and cofounder in (surprise!) a pop-up wedding

The Elopement

Elopements are not for everyone. If the idea of eloping sounds romantic, but the concept of getting married without those whom you love around you makes you feel slightly ill, then listen to your gut. But if you realize that planning a wedding is not going to work in your situation, or if your wedding plans have gotten so out of control that you don't recognize them anymore, well, elopements can be wonderful things.

The most brilliant part of eloping is that you don't have to plan it. If you decide to elope, you can toss this book aside (and come back to read Chapter 9 when all is said and done), throw your spreadsheets out the window, and go. Emily Threlkeld, who eloped to New Orleans, said that she initially tried to plan her elopement until she realized that the planned elopement was a contradiction in terms. She said, "I let things go. I turned to Google, and within the week I had ordered a dress, our wedding bands, a pair of shoes. I'd found a minister, a photographer, and a florist. I tried to find a hairdresser in New Orleans and had visions of a fabulous updo shellacked to my head with a lot of hairspray, but I ended up going with Spin Pins instead." Not only is there no planning to worry about, there are also no rules to follow. While elopements are traditionally just the couple, they don't have to be. Jessica Flaherty married in a beach town in Maine, right before Christmas, with both mothers in attendance. She told me, "We mulled the idea of elopement over for a few days and decided that despite how romantic a true dictionary definition of eloping sounded, we are both children of single moms, and our mothers meant too much to us and sacrificed too much for us both to be excluded." You're eloping because it's right for you. So for goodness' sake, if you want to bring some people you love with you, do it.

With elopements, even more than with regular weddings, you have to come face-to-face with the fact that your decisions might upset people in your lives. And that's hard. Part of getting married is forming a new family unit and prioritizing the needs of that new family. Lindsay Whitfield wrote her parents a letter explaining their choice to elope and said, "I hoped that they would understand that we were doing things in a way that was right for us." In a sense, this is true whether you elope or not. But knowing that does not make it easy to deal with hurt feelings. Jessica Flaherty said, "I am relatively unfazed, and I am still married despite the limited discontent. I appreciate that people may be disappointed to not share our day with us, but I hope they all know they were there in spirit." Even with some family displeasure, for people who went with their heart, the rewards of eloping were worth the limited pain. Lindsay Whitfield told me that even a year later, when having trouble sleeping at night, she would "replay our wedding day in my head and smile myself to sleep."

If you know in your heart of hearts that elopement is for you? Go for it. And remember that you can throw a huge party later to celebrate your marriage and that you can throw an anniversary party any year that you want to celebrate what really matters—the family that you made together.

eeee

Calling Off Your Wedding and Eloping
By Shana Xavier, of Shana Xavier Events

When I was little, I never dreamed of what my wedding would look like. I never cut out magazine pictures and glued them to a board or sketched wedding dresses. What I would picture was myself old and wrinkly, sitting next to an equally old and wrinkly person holding hands and being happy. Yes, my twelve-year-old self looked forward to the days of sitting on a couch next to her husband, crocheting and watching *Law & Order* (which may or may not describe my current relationship).

Even when we first got engaged I didn't daydream about what our wedding day would look like. Instead of imagining our first dance and centerpieces, I would daydream about all of the life adventures we would go on after the wedding—starting with the honeymoon and ending with where we would retire.

All of those thoughts took a backseat once people started asking me about the wedding. I jumped headfirst into wedding planning. I started reading wedding blogs and watching trashy wedding reality shows (sorry, not sorry). We discussed what kind of wedding we wanted (fun, laid-back, intimate, and memorable) and what details were important (good food, booze, and dancing). We also had a strict budget since we were paying for the wedding ourselves. So I started with the absolute basics that I had learned over the years from TV, movies, magazines, and the Internet.

According to what I had learned, there had to be engagement photos, a rehearsal dinner, a bridal shower, a bachelorette party, a bachelor party, a white dress, a reception dress, a tux, a hair/makeup person, someone to marry us, a pretty venue, bridesmaids, groomsmen, a flower girl, a ring bearer, a large guest list, an organized seating arrangement, hors d'oeuvres, cocktails, a three-course dinner, a gigantic cake, a DJ for a dance party, *decorations everywhere* (including, but not limited to, twinkling lights, mason jars, monogrammed everything, and handmade things), party favors, a photographer, a videographer, long vows, planned speeches, and a cute exit at the end of the night.

It didn't take long before I started to freak out and joke about eloping. To tone it down we started to cut out a few things here and there that weren't essential—a second dress, flower girl/ring bearer, three-course dinner, a fancy venue, a huge cake, a DJ, crazy decorations, a giant guest list, party favors, and a videographer.

We ended up with a backyard, 150-guest, pizza-and-beer wedding in California. Totally doable, stress-free, and easy, right? Over the next few months we started figuring out the details to make it happen—chair rentals, table rentals, porta potty rentals, generators, bridesmaid/groomsmen costumes, choosing our colors/theme, decorations, catering, alcohol, music, landscaping, the invitations, and about 1,483 more things to do. The wedding was taking over my brain, and the stress was making me feel like I was slowly dying inside. But I figured that's how all people planning a wedding felt, so I ignored it.

Until one day when I was picturing our backyard wedding bash and I realized something. I had never once imagined myself at the wedding. I had thought of the wedding in my head dozens of times, yet I never saw myself at it. I tried my hardest, but I couldn't picture myself at this magnificent, Pinterest-worthy wedding. Not only was I completely miserable during the whole wedding planning process, but the wedding had become something we never wanted in the first place. After my sixty-fourth wedding planning freak-out, we said fuck it and went back to the drawing board. We asked ourselves what we truly wanted, and it was the ideas that we had lost sight of. We quickly decided on San Francisco City Hall with twenty guests (immediate family and friends), a party bus, donuts, pizza, whiskey, and bar hopping—a.k.a. our dream wedding.

(continues)

And those life adventures I used to daydream about? Well, we decided to take an extended honeymoon this summer by going to Europe for three months.

ℓℓℓℓ

When: Can You Get Legally Married in the Morning?

The companion question to "*Where* will we have this wedding?" is of course "*When* will we have this wedding?" These days, most of us are convinced that the way to get married is to have an evening wedding followed by an all-night dance party. I, for one, wanted to dance until three a.m. in my wedding shoes on a glorious balmy night. But life caught up with me. The reality is that the most popular times to have weddings (evenings, weekends, basically any time of the year that's not winter) are also the most expensive times to have weddings. And while you hear less about them, off-season weddings, morning weddings, and weeknight weddings all have their advantages—and I don't just mean the advantage of relative affordability.

Morning and Afternoon Weddings

As someone who had a morning wedding against her will and ended up loving it, let me give you the full scoop about the nonevening wedding. There are obvious drawbacks to the morning wedding: you'll have to get up early, your prewedding preparation will be a little rushed, you won't dance the night away (at least at your reception). But there are a multitude of advantages. It's often possible to save quite a bit of money on morning weddings: you can get venues that would otherwise be booked up; you can negotiate discounts with vendors; you can serve more affordable food; people drink less alcohol. But the advantages don't stop there. The light is beautiful, and if you're getting married in a scenic spot, daylight allows you to enjoy the view. Also, it's a well-kept secret that older generations like early-in-the-day weddings. They don't need to worry about staying up late, and they will have the energy to chat with all their friends. As for the younger generation, well, if you're drinking and dancing, your friends are going to join you. But none of that compares to the magic of after the wedding. When your wedding ends at three or four in the afternoon, you have the rest of the day to bliss out with your new spouse or go bar hopping in your wedding dress (the only time in your life you'll ever have an excuse for that).

Getting Married on a Weekday

Another tried-and-true way of making a wedding more affordable is to get married on a weekday. The easiest weekday wedding usually involves a Friday-afternoon or -evening ceremony, but weddings can happen any day of the week. Weekday weddings are, however, a bit like destination weddings: when you ask people to take time off work to attend your ceremony, let them off the hook straightaway. If they can come, you'll be delighted. If they can't, you'll fully understand. That said, if you're planning a small wedding, celebrating on a weekday is a fabulous way to feel like the whole world belongs to you. With everyone at work, it's just you and your loved ones, celebrating your huge new commitment.

Off-Season Weddings

Ten years ago, when I got married, the peak of wedding season was the summer. You can blame global warming (and I do), but in that decade wedding season has extended into the fall, with the busiest wedding day of the year now falling in mid-October. This extension of wedding season means that the off-season for weddings is now, well, winter. But winter remains a very slow time for most wedding vendors, so getting married when it's cold outside can save you a sizable amount of money (on both the wedding and the honeymoon) and be beautiful. Summer

couples don't get things like tights, fir branches, hot chocolate, or snow.
And they don't get to celebrate their anniversary as a beacon of light
in a dark part of the year. And we all need more joy in the depths of
winter, right?

How: Food—No, It Doesn't Need to Be Dinner

Once you've gotten a rough count for your guest list, sorted out your
venue, and picked the date for your wedding, the next hurdle is food.
Food is expensive, and the kind of food you serve tends to set the tone
for the kind of party you're going to have (a cake-and-punch reception
is super fun but totally different from a sit-down three-course meal).

When I told my mom that I wanted to have a meal and dancing at
my wedding, she looked at me like I'd lost my mind. Forty years ago, the
only people she knew who had dinner and dancing at their reception
were fantastically wealthy. But by the time I got married, most of the
weddings I went to had sit-down meals, and I figured that was the way
to have a ragingly fun party. I was wrong. (And in the end we compro-
mised on a buffet lunch.)

My mom was right. Serving a full seated dinner is really expensive.
So, if that's not going to work for you, think about going with breakfast,
brunch, or lunch (which are often less expensive). You can serve appetizers only, or just cake and punch (which is arguably one of the *most*
traditional receptions). But beyond that, you have lots of ways that you
can source your food. You can make traditional catering work for you or
find alternative catering sources (like food trucks). No matter what tool
you use, you can absolutely find a way to serve delicious food on a budget that is right for you. Stop worrying that nothing but a steak dinner
is fun or fancy enough. "If you're catering your own wedding, and you're
worried it's gonna be a bust . . . don't," said Liz Moorhead. The people

who love you will love you no matter what you serve them, and they will show up ready to party. Your job is to figure out a way to keep yourself sane and solvent, while serving food that makes you happy.

How to Hack Traditional Catering

There are many wonderful things to be said about traditional caterers: they know what they are doing, you pay them so you never have to think about your wedding food again, they do all the setup and teardown themselves, and their food is good. (Right? Because if it's bad, you'd better not be paying them cash money.) That said, traditional catering can also feel very predictable and expensive. So if you're using traditional catering, it's important to remember that you can hack the system to make it work for you.

- Ask about less traditional food choices. Caterers are quick to recommend the meat entrée with two sides and bread because that's what most people want, but you should feel free to get creative. We had our caterer prepare a non-meat-centric Middle Eastern spread. The food was delicious and unexpected, and we were able to shave a little off the cost by not preparing pricey cuts of meat.

- Differentiate between expensive food and tasty food. There are some caterers that specialize in food-that-looks-fancy: filet mignon, anything served by waiters in black tie, wedding-cakes-as-art with a side of ice sculpture. Expect these caterers to be more expensive. There are also caterers who specialize in food that looks less fancy but is in fact super tasty. Don't be suckered into thinking that elaborate food is the best food. If you look beyond the ice sculptures, you can often find better-tasting solutions that are more affordable.

- See if you can provide some of your own extras. Your caterer may be willing to provide you with a fancy wedding cake—for a fee.

This may not be something they make in house, but something they contract a cake maker to bake for them. If so, they will charge you for the hassle. So start chatting about what extras you can provide on your own. Our caterers let us provide our own cake (and were delighted to not have to bother with it themselves), as well as our own alcohol. This saved us some serious money.

Yes, of Course Restaurants Cater

The hidden-in-plain-view secret about wedding catering is that (. . . wait for it . . .) you don't need to use a wedding caterer. If you have a venue that is flexible on catering options, you can look into getting your food from a variety of different sources, including, but not limited to, the following:

- ⇟ restaurants
- ⇟ gourmet grocery stores (party platters)
- ⇟ good carts (taco trucks, etc.)
- ⇟ pizzerias (yes, I said it)

You can get food from any restaurant or food-service establishment willing to take a large quantity order in advance. If you use this option, you will usually still need to set up and tear down the food service on your own, as well as take care of renting tables, chairs, and plates and hauling away your own trash. You save money by doing a fair amount of the work on your own. But self-catering is a lot easier when you're not doing the actual catering.

Dream It . . . Do It

When putting together the building blocks for your wedding, it's easy to get stuck. You think that you have to have a hundred people, or a dance floor, or an evening wedding, or serve dinner. Even when you realize that you just can't make your wedding fit into the prescribed vision, you keep trying to make it work because you think you don't have another choice. A wedding just *is* a big, formal, seated-dinner thing, no avoiding that fact.

But that's not true. A wedding is when you vow to spend your life with another person, and then you find a way to celebrate that. Sometimes you just need permission to dream and color outside of the celebration lines. Allow your wedding to be what it needs to be. Maybe it's a dance party in the middle of the desert; maybe it's a last-minute elopement; maybe it's planned by your partner, and nothing like what you expected. Step back, loosen the reins, and let your wedding happen. It may not look like what you imagined. It may look better.

WEDDING HOMEWORK

- Are you feeling pressured to have a particular kind of wedding? Spend some time figuring out what pressures you've internalized and write them all down. Then circle the things you actually care about and cross out the things that are not that important to you. Encourage your partner to do the same exercise. (Male partners often claim that they don't have internalized wedding bullshit, but the reality is their internalized stuff is often buried so deep, they haven't thought to question it.)
- Start working on the guest list. This means asking your families (if they're involved) whom they want to invite and figuring out whom you want to invite. Next up you need to figure out roughly how many people you want (or can have) at your wedding. Then you have to do the hard work of negotiating. So, start drawing up your lists and get that spreadsheet going.
- You have to find a wedding venue before you can buy a dress or take a serious stab at all the other fun stuff. Start to figure out if you want an all-inclusive venue or a more traditional (but not all-inclusive) venue, or if you're willing to do the work

(continues)

to get way outside the box—even if that means trash removal. That means it's research time.

○ Once you have a wedding venue, it's time to figure out food. Don't let anyone—including me—tell you what that has to look like.

○ Mantra when you start feeling overwhelmed: "Our wedding will be what we need it to be."

The Budget

ℭ —— Beyond the Spreadsheets ——୭

⁍ Research average wedding prices in your area and then talk about what you *want* to spend. These numbers do not have to be the same.

⁍ If you haven't had a heart-to-heart about how each of you feels about money, and how money has played a role in your life so far, consider discussing that now. That's a conversation you should have before you wade into spending the most money you've ever spent.

⁍ Talk with each other about if you want to accept money from family (and if your family will want to contribute). This is a great chance to discuss how each of your families approaches money and if their cash comes with strings attached.

⁍ If you and your partner are paying for the wedding yourselves, remember to take a moment to celebrate how empowering that is.

⁍ Let go of guilting yourself over how much you're spending on your wedding. Planning a wedding is stressful enough.

(continues)

You don't need to include "beating yourself up over money" on your to-do list.

⁊ Focus on all the times you hear "yes" during wedding planning. Making a joyful wedding happen on whatever budget you've got is eminently doable. Don't let people tell you otherwise.

How Much Does a Wedding Cost?

There are two basic questions you need to consider: How much does a wedding cost? And how much can we afford to spend on our wedding? While it's helpful to get an answer to the first question, try not to get it confused with the answer to the second question. In the past thirty years or so, the price of weddings in the United States (and the expectation of professionalism at weddings) has gone through the roof (for far more discussion of this, see Chapter 4). So, when you start researching average wedding budgets in your area, it's easy to become convinced that you will never be able to afford to get married, ever. So, let's just lay this out now: throwing a conventional wedding costs a lot more than you think it should. That said, you can afford to get married, no matter how much or how little you have to spend. In this chapter, we'll discuss researching wedding costs, figuring out who is going to help you pay for the wedding, getting realistic about what you can get for the money you have, putting your budget on paper, making the seemingly endless budget decisions, and having the occasional happy splurge.

Do Your Research (It's Scary, but Necessary)

There is a reason for researching average wedding prices, scary as they are. If you're not experienced at throwing events, you just don't know what they cost. And, because reality matters, you need to establish a framework before you start making plans. If the average catering cost in your area is $10,000, and you have $5,000 to spend on food, it's good to know that you will probably need to get creative and make some compromises. Maybe you'll do your research and hire an up-and-comer, or maybe you'll have a breakfast wedding. But chances are, you're not going to get the most popular joint in town for a Saturday-night lobster dinner, and the sooner you realize that, the happier you'll be.

Figure Out What You Want to Spend

Once you've researched average wedding costs in your area, you're ready to figure out your budget. Here is the most important part: trust yourself. Marie-Ève Laforte, who got married in an apple orchard outside Montreal, said, "Don't listen when anyone tells you that you simply have to spend this and that much on something. You really don't. In fact, you don't have to do anything that does not feel right to you, or that makes you feel financially uncomfortable." If the cost of something feels unsettling, chances are you shouldn't do it. Let it go. Move on and look for other options. If you're willing to compromise and be creative (not to mention ruthlessly cut things from your budget that you don't care about), you absolutely will be able to find a solution that lets you sleep at night.

Practice Constant Forgiveness

When we publish weddings on APW, we ask for the original planned budget and the actual budget. With a few exceptions (often for people who decided to radically downscale their wedding or elope), the original planned budget is usually noticeably less than the actual amount of money spent. How does that happen? The media would like you to believe that silly women (always women) get caught up in the expectations of the wedding industry and spend $10,000 on a live dove release. (Silly them. You would know better.) In reality? Wedding planner Alyssa Griffith explains it this way: "The culprits usually are something like this: The couple thought chair rentals cost $1 when they really cost $2. Or they found out that their dad would be heartbroken if they just served sandwiches. Then it turned out that the only wedding photographers in their area who didn't call them 'sweetie' during the initial meeting charged $3,000 instead of the $2,500 they were hoping to spend, and not being talked down to felt like it was worth finding an extra $500 in the budget. Next thing they knew, the combined total of those surprises was $5,000 and rising."

While I can talk to you all day about how your wedding should cost an amount that you're comfortable spending (and that for sure is true), you're also dealing with what things actually cost. And when you start multiplying costs by one hundred guests and realizing what it costs to pay vendors a living wage, your budget has a tendency to climb.

There are two ways you can deal with that. You can decide those costs are really not going to work for you and cut back. (That may mean getting creative, or it may mean scaling your wedding back from one hundred guests to seventy-five, or moving it from Manhattan to Iowa.) Or, you may choose to shrug and realize that the wedding you want costs more than you thought it would—because reality works like that sometimes—and adjust and move on.

No matter what path you take, make sure you practice constant forgiveness with yourself. There is no inherent meaning or value in the amount of money you spend on a wedding. There is only what works for you, and what really doesn't.

Putting It on Paper

When it comes to the nitty-gritty of building your wedding budget, figure out (1) what kind of wedding you want (see exercises in Chapter 1) and (2) how much money you have to spend. (Keep in mind that how much you're spending may increase or decrease as you start planning this thing. But at the end of the day, you and your partner are the ones in control of these decisions.)

Not Everything Is Equally Important

What's important to you? In Chapter 1, you and your partner worked to make a list of your wedding priorities. Now it's time to translate those priorities into a real-life spending plan. Make two lists: things you want to put more resources toward and things you want to put fewer resources toward, or not bother with at all. Be ruthless. Sure, everyone says you have to have wedding flowers, but if you don't want to spend much on flowers, put them on the Less Resources list. This doesn't mean that you won't have flowers, or that you won't spend any money on flowers. It just means that you're de-prioritizing flower spending. Maybe you'll have fake flowers, or maybe you'll use grocery-store flowers that your maid of honor will arrange for you day-of. But mostly you're not going to worry too much about flowers when you're building your budget. Think of it this way: it's better to do a few things well than to do a lot of things poorly. If you go to a wedding with a great bluegrass band and potluck food, you're just going to remember how much fun you had dancing, not that they didn't have fancy food. So put your money toward a few items that are worth it to you, and don't worry too much about the rest.

However, try to avoid falling into the trap of believing that how much you spend on something indicates how much you care about it. Sometimes items that didn't top your priority list end up being things you spend more on. There are times in wedding planning when you will think, "I do not care about this thing, and I will rip out my eyes if I have to think about it for one more second. Hence, I will throw money at it." Or, as Kimberly Eclipse, who married on Long Island, New York, said, "Sometimes, money is just numbers on paper. If there was something that we really wanted, or felt that we needed to do, then we paid for it. No, I didn't want to go above a certain amount, but that arbitrary amount became less important than what it paid for." There are times you'll want to pay money to make a problem go away.

And sometimes the things that you care the most about are the things that cost the least: a dress that you made yourself, the toasts people made around the table, the time you spent with your mom putting together your flowers. Sometimes *how* we spend our money is more important than *how much of it* we spend. If you buy affordable fabric to make your wedding dress with your mom, but then throw a thousand dollars at hiring a day-of coordinator so you don't ever have to think about logistics again, that's a great choice.

No, You Don't Have to Add It Up

Or you can take the exact opposite tack and add nothing up. The trouble with wedding budgets is they can take on an emotional life of their own. Spend enough time reading about reasonably priced weddings, and you'll start tying your pride to your budget number. You'll think, "I'm having a $10,000 wedding, damn it, and not a penny more," and then the week before the wedding when you figure out that you have $2,000 in plane ticket expenses that you didn't see coming, you'll find yourself a sobbing mess on the floor as you try to explain to your partner that you had a budget number in mind, and what are you going to do now that you're over that budget?

So, in these moments of temporary insanity, it's important to remember that you're not reporting your final budget to anyone. You're likely not publishing it on the Internet; you're not passing it out to your friends; you're not telling total strangers. What you spend is your business, and after the wedding is over, you're going to find out it doesn't matter very much. So add it up creatively if it makes you feel better. Or don't add it up at all.

Or, heck, don't have a budget in the first place. Kirsten Duke, who got married on her neighbor's property in Ontario, Canada, found that "not having a budget kept me sane. I got an influx of cash in December, so we started planning around that. From that point, we spent money on the wedding whenever we had extra out of our paychecks, and from gifts from our parents and grandparents. I honestly to this day have no idea what we spent. I have an approximate idea, but in the end the system that worked best for us was to just continually move forward." If you tend to operate in a more freewheeling fashion, or if a wedding budget is going to make you feel obsessive and bordering on insane, it's perfectly responsible to just try to spend an amount that feels sensible to you on each item. You're two fully grown adults. You can absolutely throw a wedding with no formal budget but with a lot of common sense.

> If I could go back and change anything, I would have opened a checking account specifically for the wedding in the very beginning of planning. Between my husband and I moving money back and forth and money coming in from different family members, I never knew how much money I actually had to live life during planning.
>
> —Sarah Huck, who had a feminist disco spectacular at the all-pink Madonna Inn in San Luis Obispo, California

Sample Wedding Budgets (to Inspire You)
By Alyssa Griffith

The most important thing to remember when you're putting together your budget is that no two weddings are alike. Your budget, and how money is allocated, is fluid and will undoubtedly change and need adjusting throughout the planning process. But what kinds of weddings can you actually throw at various price points? Where can you get creative with the money you've got? To answer those questions, here's a broad overview of what some different wedding budgets might look

(continues)

like in practice. While these are meant to serve as sample wedding budgets, they come from years of seeing real couples plan weddings on similar budgets in similar circumstances. These budgets are not meant to limit you, but instead to help you start brainstorming ideas. Mix and match. Let them inspire you. Forget the hotel wedding (unless, of course, you want the hotel wedding!); wedding ideas come in all shapes and sizes.

A $2,000 City Hall Elopement/Super-Small Wedding

Venue/officiant: $150 for a thirty-minute slot at city hall for you and up to 6 guests, officiant included

Attire: $200 dress; $100 suit

Flowers: $100 for one bouquet and one boutonnière

Photographer: $800 for a quick one-hour session of ceremony plus portraits

Delicious restaurant lunch and drinks for 8: $600

Grand total: $1,950

A $2,000 Backyard Dessert Party

Venue: $0

Invites: $0 evites

Officiant (family/friend): $30 to be ordained

Flowers and decor: $250 DIY

Rentals: $300 for a few supplemental chairs, tables, and linens

Dessert for 50: $200, plus donated by family and friends

Photographer: $1,000

Champagne and iced tea for 50: $200

Casual backyard party attire: $100

Music: $0 for iPod and borrowed speakers

Grand Total: $2,080

A $5,000 Backyard Food Truck Extravaganza

Venue: $0

Attire: $200 for two dresses; $50 for shoes

Invites: $80, DIY-ed (don't forget about stamps!)

Decor: $800 for string lights, flowers, and table and chair rentals

Flowers: $200 for two bridal bouquets and two smaller bouquets

Catering: $2,000 for delicious food truck eats for 50 people (including compostable dishware)

Beer and wine: $500

Dessert: $300 for pies from a local bakery

Music: $150 for a streaming music service, your 17-year-old cousin/aspiring DJ, and rented speakers

Photography: $500, by a local art student

Grand total: $4,780

A $10,000 Outdoor Venue with a Full Meal

Venue: $2,200, including chairs and tables

DJ: $800

Food and alcohol: $3,800 (sample how-to: restaurant-delivered food or affordable catering at $30 per person, booze at $20 per person, with 75 guests)

Attire: $350 dress; $150 suit

Decor: $500 for string lights purchased on sale and DIY flowers

Photographer: $1,200

Day-of wedding coordinator: $900

Dessert: $250 for cupcakes

Grand total: $10,150

The $10,000 Midday Party with the Dream Dress

Venue: $1,100 (12:30 p.m. ceremony, 1:00 p.m. cocktails and appetizers, 5:30 p.m. end time)

Rentals: $800 for chairs and a few cocktail tables plus linens

Attire: $1,200 dress and shoes; $200 suit

Invitations: $300

Catering and alcohol: $3,500, including heavy appetizers served from 1:00 p.m. to 4:00 p.m.

Cake: $500

Photographer: $2,000

Music: $200 for a live guitarist during the ceremony; $200 for rented speakers plus iPhone

(continues)

Decor: $150 for one bouquet and one boutonniere from a professional; $300 for DIY centerpiece flowers
Grand total: $10,250

A $15,000 Art Gallery All-Night Party

Venue: $800 (you can often save a ton by thinking outside the wedding venue box)
Rentals: $1,500 for chairs, tables, linens, and basic lighting
Attire: $700 dress and shoes; $250 suit
Alcohol: $900
Catering: $5,000 for a full buffet plus a late-night snack
DJ: $2,000
Photographer: $3,000
Decor: $500 for candles spread around the space
Planning: $500 for consulting with a wedding planner to ensure the details are in place
Grand total: $15,150

The $15,000 Intimate Hawaii Extravaganza

Venue: $7,000 for a house for the weekend
Rentals: $800 for tables, chairs, linens, and lights for 35 people
Catering: $3,900 for a full meal for 35 people
Alcohol: $700, self-purchased
Invitations: $75, using an online service and evites
Attire: Two rented suits at $200 each
Photographer: $2,500
Cake: $400
Music: $0, DIY-ed by a friend
Flowers: $0, greenery and flowers from the Hawaii landscape
Grand total: $15,775

A $20,000 Brooklyn Bash

Venue and full-service catering: $12,000, including food, alcohol, tables, chairs, and service staff for 55 guests
Photography: $2,000
Wedding planner: $2,000
Invitations: $800
Attire: $800 dress; $150 suit
Flowers and decor: $1,200

DJ: $1,000
Grand total: $19,950

The $20,000 Barn Party

Venue: $1,000
Full-service catering: $10,000 for food, alcohol, rentals, and staff for 120 guests
Wedding planner: $2,000
Photographer: $3,000
Flowers: $2,000
Attire: $1,100 dress; $200 suit
DJ: $1,200
Grand total: $20,500

A $30,000 Big Church Ceremony with Hotel Party to Follow

Church/ceremony rental: $400
Wedding planner: $2,800
Reception venue and full-service catering: $17,000, including all food, alcohol, rentals, and staff for 140 guests
Flowers: $2,500
Photography and videography: $4,000
Attire: $1,400 dress; $250 suit
Live band: $3,000
Grand total: $31,350

A $30,000 Mountain Weekend Retreat

Venue: $6,000 for a whole weekend at a summer camp in the woods
Attire: $600 dress; $140 suit
Friday-night potluck: $800 for alcohol and appetizers
Saturday breakfast and lunch: $3,000
Music: $500 live strings during ceremony; $1,200 DJ
Saturday-night full-service catering: $10,000, including all food and alcohol
Decor: $3,000 for flowers and extra rental items
Sunday-morning brunch: $2,000

(continues)

Photographer: $2,800
Grand total: $30,040

Try to remember—while having a budget is important, helpful, and downright necessary in the wedding planning process, what's really important is that you and your partner end up somewhere with all of your favorite people (or none of your favorite people), committing yourselves to each other, and starting a marriage.

꙾꙾꙾꙾

Who Pays? (And What Does That Mean?)

There are as many different configurations of people paying for a wedding as there are families. Your first step is to figure out if you want to ask loved ones to help contribute to your wedding funds. Keep in mind—people who contribute money are going to feel like they have a legitimate involvement in the project that is your wedding. While it's up to you to set boundaries on what that level of involvement will be, the first thing to consider is who you want involved in the first place. If you have a difficult relationship with your family, or if you want to call all the shots yourself, let that influence your decision.

You may also find yourself in a situation where you have family that very much want to contribute and participate in wedding planning, but simply can't afford to chip in financially. In that case, we'll talk about ways for you to let them feel involved—because even though this chapter is all about budgets, money isn't everything.

Your Family Is Helping to Pay

Talking to Your Family

Before you walk into a conversation with your family about contributing financially to the wedding, make sure you have a pretty good idea of what kind of wedding you're throwing (at least tentatively). It's not fair to ask your parents to help pay for what they think is a Catholic Mass wedding, only to surprise them with the pagan-handfasting-in-a-meadow plan after they've written a check. Have several long talks with your partner and do your research so you are prepared for the conversation with your family. A fair conversation is one that starts with the facts. "We're thinking of doing a secular wedding service followed by a lunch reception. We think the price will be somewhere between $10,000 and $25,000, depending on the location and the length of the guest list. Let's talk about what your preferences are, and then you can think about how much (and if) you'd like to contribute financially."

Next up, you need to talk about how much your parents can contribute—realistically. Remember, by this point in the process, you've gotten a good idea of what weddings cost, and your parents may have no idea (and if they're assuming wedding costs are comparable to twenty years ago, they might end up shell-shocked). So lay out your projection of expenses and then let them think it over.

Then, talk specific numbers. Money is hard to talk about, so it's easy to get sucked into the land of vague. "Sure," they say, "we'll pay for the venue, within reason." It may feel like a struggle to nail down real numbers now, but it's going to be a lot more awkward telling them you just booked a venue that is three times the cost of what they expected to pay. While you're asking difficult questions, find out *when* your parents' money will be arriving. Maybe they can hand you a check right away. Maybe they can hand you a check the day before the wedding. While you should be grateful in both circumstances, they represent very different cash-management strategies, so make sure you know up front.

And here is the kicker: make sure they are offering you money that they can afford to offer. Brides' parents in particular sometimes have an emotional need to pay for their daughters' weddings. This may lead to parents offering cash that they really need for retirement or bills, which is no good. The same rule that holds true for your wedding spending holds true for your parents' wedding spending—if it doesn't feel right, it probably isn't right. And no one should cash out their retirement for a party . . . even a really nice, very important party.

> It's important to note that I planned our wedding with my divorced parents. First off, they are the best divorced parents ever. But in terms of money, their finances are *obviously* separate. My advice to anyone who is getting married and has divorced parents who would like to contribute is to sit down with your parents (without their new spouses, if they exist), seriously talk about what people are willing to pay for, and write it down. I found that worked well for us. I basically said, "This is what I can afford, and this is what I picture my wedding to be like. I am not asking you to pay for my wedding, but if you would like to contribute, I just need to know who is paying for what." Just asking for what I needed to know in a very blunt way avoided a lot of miscommunication and stress.
>
> —Casey Foster, who had more bridesmaids than
> you could imagine at her wedding in Maine

Ways for People to Contribute

If one or both of your families are helping to pay for your wedding (or, heck, totally paying for your wedding), there are a number of ways to handle contributions that feel fair.

- **The even split**—It may be sensible to split your wedding budget evenly among contributors. We split our wedding budget into fourths: my parents paid for 25 percent, my husband's parents paid for 25 percent, and each of us paid for another 25 percent from our savings. There are as many ways to divide budgets as there are families, but the even split has the advantage of making everyone feel like an equal contributor. Also, it prevents any one person from feeling like they can call the shots.

≷ **Based on timing**—Think of this as the cash-flow solution to the problem. If one party has access to money now (say, your parents), and another party is still saving to help pay for the wedding (say, you), you can divide payments by timing. Your parents pay for all the up-front costs, like deposits, and you pay for all the late-in-the-game costs, like catering.

≷ **Based on interest**—It may be that your parents really care about what wedding venue you end up with or what food you serve. In that case, they may want to pay for your venue and food. Or maybe they don't have a whole lot of cash to contribute, but your mom really wants to buy your dress. In this case, it might make sense to divide the wedding budget up by item. Be aware, however, that if your parents are paying for a specific item, they will probably expect to have a say on that aspect of the wedding.

≷ **From each, according to ability**—Perhaps what feels fair to you is having people give according to what they've got. If your husband's parents are well off, and your parents are struggling, $5,000 from your parents may be as meaningful as $50,000 from his family. If you take this route, it might be wise to keep each person's contribution private. "She gave a meaningful amount" is all anyone needs to know.

Setting Planning Boundaries

While it's important to know what kind of wedding you might want before having the budget conversation with your parents, it's also important to be ready to listen to what your parents want (which we discussed in more detail in Chapter 1). But make sure to establish, from the get-go, that money does not buy influence and that everyone is in this project together.

Establish boundaries and expectations for wedding planning early. If you want your mom to go with you to every vendor meeting and help you agonize over colors, tell her now. If you are going to make some decisions without the influence of your parents, be up front about it. People who are sinking large sums of cash into your wedding will, understandably, care about the process, and you should tell them what to expect.

It's also important to respect your families' contributions, no matter how you plan the party. The money your parents are putting into the wedding is money that they worked hard for and money they could be spending on a nice vacation or paying down their mortgage. Treat it with the same respect that you would your own hard-earned money.

Oh, the Guilt

Once your family has offered money, your job is to accept it with a healthy mix of love and gratitude. It's easy to get sucked up in the guilt of accepting money and lose track of the fact that your wedding is an important milestone in which your family wants to be involved to show their love and support for you. For them, that might mean writing you a check. Katie Pegher told me that when she was worrying for the millionth time over the money they were being given, her fiancé's stepmother "threw the paperwork on the dashboard and looked me square in the eye. 'I make a damn good living,' she said, 'and I *want* to do this.'" So as hard as it can be to accept money, let it go. Your wedding is not all about you, and if you don't personally earn every penny that's spent on it, that's just fine.

You Are Paying

Perhaps you're paying for your wedding on your own. Maybe you feel terrified by the responsibility. Maybe you feel relieved that you're in control. Regardless, realize how empowering this is. You're doing this thing on your own, and that is worth celebrating.

The advantages to paying for a wedding on your own are clear—you're paying for all of it, so you get to kindly outvote pushy family members. But there is a catch—your family might not be helping you pay, but they may really want to be involved in your wedding. So ask them to participate in a way that's meaningful to them. Maybe your mom comes wedding dress shopping with you; maybe she makes the programs; maybe she just holds your hand as you freak out before you walk down the aisle. But just like paying for a wedding doesn't equal control over a wedding, not paying for a wedding doesn't negate involvement. Even if she didn't pay for a dollar of the party, chances are that your mom still wants to be your mom as you wend your way through this important life transition.

Sane Budget Rules

Once you have your wedding budget set, you've moved past theory and into practice. And practice is tricky. With that in mind, here are some rules for decision making that will keep you reasonably sane (considering):

No guilt—Trust yourself. You decided on a budget that you can afford, so let yourself spend that money without guilting yourself every step of the way. (And you know what? If you decide to go over budget, don't guilt yourself over that either.) You're lucky enough to have a chunk of money to put into the economy and to support businesses and artisans whose work you value. That's a blessing, so stop wasting your energy on guilt.

No second-guessing—Once you make a financial decision that feels right to you, stick to your guns. Wedding planning can be a constant pattern of questioning your own judgment, and this will drive you mad. If your choice was right for you, that's it. You're done, and you're fine.

Yes, Paying for a Wedding Sucks

There. It needed to be said. Weddings are expensive. And while you're in the middle of it, writing check after check after check, it can feel abjectly terrible. If you find yourself thinking, "Why are we doing this?" and "Is it going to be worth it?" and "Maybe we should just elope so we don't have to pay these bills" over and over again, know that you're in the best kind of company.

I've spoken to countless couples after they pulled off their wedding, and the vast majority report that what they spent felt worth it. And no matter how it feels, it will have the remarkable advantage of being over. The checks will be written, the wedding will be a joyful day in your memory, and you'll realize that you never have to spend that money ever again. And that will feel like freedom.

> We bought a dope neon sign that said, "Tequila Over Boys," which cost more than our dresses combined. #WorthIt
>
> —Sami Cromelin and Brit Barron, who married each other at a super-hip nontraditional venue in Los Angeles

~~~~

Unapologetic Is a Great Way to Feel About Your Wedding Budget

I spent eighteen months planning my wedding live online. I also spent eighteen months feeling eaten up inside with pure irrational guilt over my wedding budget. There was no way to talk sense into me (I know, because folks tried). It didn't matter how much people told me that feeding 120 people just cost good money. I still felt terrible. Why? Because I could have done it for less. And 100 percent guaranteed, if I had been calling all the shots at that party, I would have spent less cash.

But I wasn't planning alone. I had two sets of families with different opinions and requirements. I had a partner who also had some strong feelings. And then on top of it all, I had a couple of things I actually wanted myself.

When you're in the middle of wedding planning, the world can seem like it's divided into two camps. One camp is folks who (at least from the outside) give the impression that money is simply not an issue. And the other camp is people bragging about how little they spent on their wedding.

All these years later, I can tell you this: every second I spent feeling badly about how much we were spending on our wedding was a second wasted. It was energy I really needed for the actual problems of wedding planning, thrown down the hole of imagining what other people thought about me . . . or, worse, judging myself.

Like every other human who's ever thrown a wedding, I was working with a particular set of advantages and limitations. I had a particular number of people that we wanted to host. I had style requirements from family. I had a budget available to me that I couldn't go over, because we just flat out didn't have any more money than that to spend. So we did what every other human who's thrown a wedding has done: we made it work.

(continues)

And all these years later, I can tell you that I don't regret what we spent. Hell, I almost never even think about the amount of money we spent. Because we did what worked at the time. We had a lovely wedding, and . . . honestly? That's all that really matters.

But I also know that it can be nearly impossible to not feel consumed by guilt over your wedding budget when you're in the thick of planning. Are you spending too much? Are you spending too little? Are you asking too much of your friends and family?

We all know that one of the ways society eats away at women is by telling them all of their choices are wrong. We're consumed with guilt over what we eat, what we wear, how we parent, and on and on and on. But we don't always notice when society is giving us the same messages about weddings. We're cheap or tacky if we spend too little. We're immoral and lavish if we spend too much. We're bridezillas if the enormous massive stress put on us while planning a wedding . . . stresses us out.

And it's all bullshit. Whatever you're spending on your wedding is probably just the right amount for you. Ignore all of the messaging that says you're doing it wrong. Because you're doing it just right.

Or at the very least, you're doing it the best you know how. And what else can you ask of yourself?

ℓℓℓℓ

Somehow, Everything Is Possible

If you have a limited budget, you're going to hear a lot of "can't" and "won't be able to." But people have been having weddings with not a lot of money since time immemorial, and so much more is possible than you imagine. Once you've said yes to having a wedding, it's your job to say yes to the people around you who want to help. Stop listening to the people who tell you "no" and start paying attention when people tell you "yes." Your best friend wants to make you a wedding cake? Yes! Your parents' church will let you use the social hall for free? Yes! Your sister will loan you her wedding dress? Yes! A nonprofessional cake can be tasty, and you can make a church social hall look cute, and your wedding dress can be meaningful *and* stylish. You will be able to make your wedding what you need it to be with the elements you have available to you.

> The largest allocation by far was to the venue—the University Club in San Francisco. The largest part of that bill was the bar tab. "Your friends are drunks," we each said to each other simultaneously as we looked at the final bill. We made the decision the bar would be open. Our friends and family mean everything to us, and they took the time from their lives, and many traveled to be with us for this night, so if they wanted a drink, or four, who are we to say no?
>
> —Matt Browne, who married his husband
> in a glam San Francisco wedding

There Are No Pockets in a Shroud

When all is said and done, weddings are not about money. In the depths of planning, weddings can feel like they are about nothing but cold hard cash, but that's not true. Weddings are about love, and family, and a major life transition. They're also about things like logistics and enjoying yourself. And sometimes that costs money. Jen Smith summed it up well when she said, "Peace of mind isn't a splurge. Color-coordinated choreographed doves that launch fireworks are a splurge. Depending on your priorities, hiring a DJ might be a splurge or it might be the most important purchase. Only you will know." So, when you realize that getting a DJ will make the party for you, or that those expensive red shoes will give you a feeling of explosive joy? Sometimes it's worth it to just do it.

The amount of money you spend on your wedding doesn't have a deeper meaning. It doesn't make you a better person. It's just a number. It's just dollar bills. And as Granny will tell you, there are no pockets in a shroud. You're getting married, damn it. Life is short. Enjoy it.

· ·

WEDDING HOMEWORK

○ Do your research about average wedding costs in your area. Do online research, but also ask people you know who recently got married to talk honestly with you about costs. Ask what surprised them the most about their budget and what they would do differently if they had to do it all over again. And remember #NoJudgment. You'll be surprised how much people who just got hitched want to talk about it all, money included (if they know you're not going to judge them).

○ Start doing the math on what you have available to spend and what you *want* to spend. Talk to family members and loved ones who might want to contribute to the wedding. When you do this, get a sense of both how much money they want to contribute and what strings (or expectations) might be attached. Decide what you can live with before you take the money.

○ Start looking at the kind of wedding you want and the budget you have available to you. Do the two line up? If not, start thinking about what you need to change to make it work (better now than when you run out of money halfway through planning).

○ Remember in Chapter 1 where I had you come up with a list of what's important to you? Go back to that list and decide what you want to spend more money on (remember, it's often smart to spend money on things you need, but never want to think about again), what you want to spend less money on, and what you want to cut from the list altogether.

○ Mantra when the stress and guilt and general suckiness of writing a million checks starts to get to you: "No pockets in a shroud." Life is short. Enjoy this moment.

{ 4 }

Battling the Myth of "Tradition"

 Beyond the Spreadsheets

- When people tell you about wedding "traditions," be wary. While the basic outline of American weddings remains relatively unchanged since the 1920s, over the past few decades the size, cost, and professionalism of weddings have drastically increased.
- Figure out which traditions mean something to you and your loved ones, and don't worry about the rest.
- Remember the basic rules of wedding etiquette: be kind, be thoughtful, be honest, and don't put yourself into crushing debt to pretend you're someone you're not for five hours.
- Weddings are a great time to discuss what we believe with our partners. Have a conversation with each other about your values and beliefs around weddings. Remember that we do ourselves a great disservice when we allow tradition to be the things that we are sold instead of the things that have meaning in our hearts.

It Didn't Used to Be This Way

In many key ways, the American wedding has remained unchanged for more than a hundred years. On the surface, our weddings look remarkably similar to weddings as they were celebrated in, say, the 1920s. We have the white dresses, the tiered wedding cakes, and the catered receptions. But in rather profound ways, weddings have been in a state of flux for the last century and have drastically changed in the past few generations. While they've grown in size, they've positively metastasized when it comes to cost and effort.

Interestingly, most of the significant changes in the American way of tying the knot have been made opaque. There is a multibillion-dollar industry devoted to telling us that things have always been exactly the way they are this second and we need to buy everything on offer because "this is the way it's always been done" and "changing things would be thumbing our nose at tradition and all the generations that have gone before us." The thing is, this is not strictly true.

I think it's empowering to know a little bit about wedding history. That way, when you hear the word *tradition*, you'll have a sense of whether what's being referred to is, in fact, traditional (say, the vows) or is brand-new (say, the unity candle). This will make you much better equipped to take all advice with a grain of salt (or to say, "Actually, Mom, we don't *need* an aisle runner . . .").

Also, it turns out that actual wedding etiquette is remarkably uninterested in your spending boatloads of money. (Who knew?) The goal of this chapter is to help you reclaim *actual* tradition, in a way that's helpful to you.

A Note on the Diversity of Weddings

It's important to mention that while our cultural narrative in the United States tends to center around white people, that is just one fraction of the weddings that have taken place in this country and on this land. While it's true that American brides didn't by and large go for short skirts till the 1920s or have a Charles and Diana–style lavish wedding till the 1980s, that shouldn't erase the major differences in how weddings have always been performed. While in this chapter I chart the wider wedding trends as practiced in the mainstream of the United States, I specifically want to highlight wedding traditions during the time of slavery.

Many of us take for granted the fact that our ability to freely get married is a privilege, and it's important to recognize that fact. This same story can be traced across many communities in the United States. *Loving v. Virginia*—which recognized the constitutional right of interracial couples to legally marry—happened as recently as 1967. And the *Obergefell v. Hodges* ruling—which recognized the constitutional rights of the Queer community to legally wed—came down in 2015, several years after I wrote the first edition of this book. (Cue the confetti cannons!) As a country we are deeply imperfect and often late to honoring the rights of all human beings to marry. But our greatest strength is our complex mix of peoples, joining together to create new families.

Our own wedding meshed White Protestant traditions with Ashkenazi Jewish wedding practices. And at its best, this is what makes American weddings great. Our traditions span so many cultures, and we are able to hold all of that diversity in one country, and sometimes even in one wedding.

A Brief History of Weddings in America

The Un-Fussy 1800s

Let's start in the early 1800s in the United States. Most weddings during this period took place at home (meaning your at-home or backyard wedding is perhaps the most traditional wedding that you could possibly throw). There were a variety of different reasons that weddings took place in the home. For middle-class Protestants, the feeling was that the ritual of marriage should not be fussy and glorified, but rather simple and held in a place with emotional significance to the parties involved. And for much of the population, there was limited access to churches to get married *in*. So, the at-home wedding was the standard, and these celebrations were generally quiet, small, and informal. These weddings were planned with very little lead time and generally very little expense. A few weeks' notice was given, the bride wore her best (and not usually white) dress, the family gathered, vows were said, and cake was eaten.

By the mid-nineteenth century, life in America started to become slightly more ritualized. Wedding ceremonies began moving to churches, making them both more formal and more expensive. Wedding receptions, by and large, were still held at home. It's important to note that at this point in our cultural history, weddings were not parties thrown by professionals. The women in the family were still doing it all—the cooking, the decorating, and often even the sewing of the wedding dress. In fact, most women would have been horrified at the idea of hiring help to do something that was seen as a labor of love. These days, we talk about DIY weddings as if they were a newfangled wedding trend, but the fact of the matter is that weddings historically were do-it-together events. Weddings were viewed as deeply personal celebrations, not to be mucked about with by professionals (and besides, there was great pride in throwing your daughter a party to celebrate this huge transition in her life).

Weddings During Slavery

But it's important to note that during most of the 1800s, slavery was still alive and well in the United States. Part of the brutality of slavery was complete control of the most intimate familial relationships. Enslaved people had no legal right to marry, and enslaved men had no paternal rights. Still, weddings happened, even with the constant threat of forcible separation from loved ones. As cited in the *New York Times* on August 1, 2011, vows were not "Till death do us part," but were sometimes put as bluntly as "Till the white man do us part."

The ritual of marriage varied during the antebellum period, from plantation to plantation, from those enslaved in the house to those enslaved in the fields. One of the most consistent rituals, however, was the jumping of the broom. This ritual was revived by descendants of slaves in the 1970s to serve as a powerful emotional reminder of freedoms gained from ancestors' struggles. Today it's common to see Black descendants of slaves in the United States incorporate jumping the broom into their wedding ceremonies as a means of recognizing their culture and forbears.

The Turn of the Century, and the Beginnings of the Professional Wedding

Professional wedding services began to make an appearance at the turn of the century, but in ways that we wouldn't even recognize now. Making your cake and then sending it to a baker to be professionally decorated? Now we would think of that as DIY and crafty. But at the turn of the century, this was a huge step in the direction of professionalism. As invitations began to be purchased (newfangled!) and lavish public weddings held by the wealthy became increasingly common, the commercialization of weddings became something of a flash point. Was simple better? Were people losing connection with tradition in favor of showy weddings that parted families from their hard-earned money? It seems that when it comes to grand old wedding traditions, the fight to bring back simple weddings is as traditional as anything else (and more traditional than the aisle runner).

The Flappers Bring Us the Wedding Industry (Kind Of)

Oddly, it was during the rebellious, hard-drinking, short skirt– and lipstick-wearing 1920s that the wedding industry as we know it became visible. During this period of massive social change, an industry was born that marketed weddings as traditional, unchanging, and profoundly conservative. If your daughter is going to get married in a shockingly short, knee-length skirt and smoke and drink at her reception, it's reassuring to be told how to make her wedding proper. The wedding industry that developed in the 1920s had very little to do with the actual history of the small at-home weddings thrown with little to no professional help. But during an era of change, the idea of "traditional" weddings had an undeniable appeal.

In fact, what emerged in the 1920s was a wedding that bears a lot of resemblance to the weddings that we see today. For the first time, most weddings took place in churches, and the receptions moved out of the home and into public social halls. Dancing began to be part of the festivities, along with photography, and the white wedding dress became readily available (off the rack!) to a wide swath of American women. It's a classic chicken-and-egg question: Did the modern wedding industry give birth to the more complicated, more expensive wedding, or is it the other way around? Regardless, with a generation of women marrying in white, something that their mothers did not do, brides and mothers needed advice. And as would become a constant, the wedding industry was there to provide advice. Expensive advice. Advice about mostly invented tradition. Expensive tradition.

Love Knows No Depression

As the roaring 1920s became the depressed 1930s, you would think that the newly formed wedding industry would go into hibernation. But, as one of the slogans of the time read, "Love knows no depression!" Thanks to some rather serious marketing efforts, in the 1930s the white wedding became the standard template for weddings and was increasingly available to everyone. In a time of very little money and very little waste, women were buying white wedding dresses that could be reworn but (with a brief interlude of wartime civil ceremonies excepted) that didn't last long.

The Wartime Courthouse Wedding

And then the war years dawned. With so many men heading off to fight in World War II, marriage rates skyrocketed. Eighty percent of the grooms were in the armed services, so civil ceremonies became a necessity. When your groom is shipping off to war in a week, you hurry down to the courthouse in your best suit or dress (with flowers), celebrate with some punch and cake, and then dash off to spend some time alone. But the wedding industry wasn't going to let everyone off quite that easily (after all, an industry that had survived the Depression could make it through a war). Suddenly, the rhetoric surrounding weddings changed. The white wedding became deeply patriotic—part of the American way of life everyone was fighting for.

The Traditional 1950s

As the war ended and we moved toward the deeply conservative 1950s, it is hardly surprising that weddings got bigger, more formal, and more expensive. In her excellent wedding history book, *All Dressed in White*, Carol McD. Wallace sums up the era this way: "The wedding ceased to be a homemade celebration and became something you bought." She explains, "In the mid-twentieth century . . . what was once optional becomes obligatory." The language of the modern wedding industry emerged, and the wedding became "your big day" and "once in a lifetime." And if it's once in a lifetime, it of course needs to be done *properly*. As the 1950s and 1960s rolled on, "properly" quickly came to mean a big white dress, an elaborate church wedding, and a lavish catered reception. Though, interestingly enough, the lavish catered reception in the mid-twentieth century consisted of tea sandwiches and cake, something that today's wedding industry would tell us Cannot Be Done.

Barefoot and Pregnant in a (Personalized) Field

During the mid-twentieth century, bigger became bigger became bigger, and then the counterculture 1970s arrived. Marriage became a highly individual choice, not a necessity. People began wanting weddings to illustrate the deepest longings of their soul. Couples began to eschew every form of perceived tradition and got married barefoot and pregnant in a meadow. But strangely enough, while everyone was distracted with counterculture celebrations, mainstream weddings suddenly became more complicated.

You see, if weddings are about the deepest desires of our souls, then they should be personalized. It was in the 1970s that wedding favors were introduced, along with the unity candle. Within the span of ten years, the recommended time for wedding planning expanded from six months to, in 1973, a full year. Which was perfect, because around the same time that getting married in a field became old hat, the 1980s hit. After Diana and Charles's spectacle of a big-sleeved, fairy-tale royal wedding, weddings got enormous. Conspicuous. Expensive. And we started to inch closer to what weddings were to become: a mind-bogglingly expensive, not even vaguely traditional production.

Modern Weddings

That brings us to the most complicated and commercial production of all: the modern wedding. Over the past hundred years, one thing has stayed consistent: the accumulation of tradition. We have continued to invent and add rituals, but we almost never subtract them. We started with the cake, vows, and decorations and slowly added things like the white dress, the double-ring ceremony, bridal bouquets, wedding parties, catered receptions, dancing, and photography. And in the past thirty years, things have gotten ever more complex and expensive. In the 1970s, weddings started moving toward personalization. These days, everything is personalized, and everything *means* something. You can't just serve tea sandwiches; you have to think about what serving tea sandwiches says about you. And then you have to research online all the possible kinds of tea sandwiches that you could serve and think about how to style them. Nothing is simple, and the Internet is there to provide us with endless information, which is fun, right till it slowly drives us insane.

And, of course, you can't serve tea sandwiches in the first place. As Carol McD. Wallace notes in *All Dressed in White*, "The basic elements of the wedding have been ramped up in the last twenty years. A seated dinner at the reception is now the norm, rather than passed hors d'oeuvres or a buffet. Since very few couples today feel the need to rush off to consummate their relationship, wedding receptions tend to last longer, often involving dancing, and there may be a brunch the next day as well, attended by the couple. In today's mobile society, families and guests often travel long distances for a wedding, so there is distinct pressure to make the event worth their while." In short, weddings have become enormous. We are trying to function under the weight of a hundred years of invented traditions, piled one on top of the other. Each new tradition is invented by an ever-bigger, ever-stronger wedding industry, ready to tell us that we will regret it if we give up any aspect of the ever-larger wedding.

ౖౖౖౖ

My Parents' 1974 Fancy Yet Practical Wedding— as Written by My Dad, Fred Keene

Hannah and I got married at the high altar in Grace Cathedral in San Francisco with five Episcopal priests celebrating the Eucharist early in the winter on the Feast of the Holy Innocents.

Elaborate, yes. Expensive, not really. The five priests were close personal friends, most about our age. We asked them to wear their fanciest, most colorful vestments. A friend printed

(continues)

copies of the liturgy so everybody knew what to say. I asked my brother to be head usher; the other ushers and our attendants were close friends. We chose the hymns and even included a Christmas carol. Other friends baked the bread for Communion. We chose a Zinfandel for the wine and asked the priests to give big sips to the recipients. The wedding ceremony itself takes no more than twenty minutes, so we chose to have Communion. It is optional but emphasizes the idea that a wedding incorporates a married couple into the community. We are big on that kind of thing.

The Christmas decorations were still up in the cathedral; the only flowers we needed were corsages for our mothers and bouquets for Hannah and her attendants. We did not belong to the cathedral congregation, so the use of the building cost a couple hundred dollars, but a verger—a custodian, wearing vestments—came with it. We decided to hire one of the cathedral organists for another hundred or two. This did not seem like very much, and he could play anything we wanted, including, for the recessional, some heavy-duty Bach that matched one of the hymn tunes. We had the receiving line at the back of the church so we could greet our friends, and they could start partying as soon as they got to the reception. The organist rang change for half an hour. The photographer had shot my sister's wedding two years earlier—the reception had been in my parents' backyard—and charged us the same price even though he was from out of town and had to travel. (His wife wanted an excuse for a trip to San Francisco.)

Hannah did all the heavy lifting in putting the wedding together. In the late spring she had agreed to marry me, so she had about six months. I had just finished my degree, and my first full-time job was on the East Coast. It started in late August, so I was not around to help her. Both of her parents worked full-time, so although they paid for the wedding and set some limits, the wedding belonged to Hannah. However, I was around when she got her wedding dress in the early summer. It was a winter dress with long sleeves, and was marked down 50 percent to $150 at one of the high-end department stores, which fit right into the budget. The dress was actually a little short and could not be lengthened, so Hannah wore perfectly flat ballet-style satin bedroom slippers to disguise the shortness.

Hannah's parents arranged for the reception; the ceremony was ours. The reception cost more than $1,000, a lot of money in those days, but it covered the venue, the food, and the setup and service. We served hors d'oeuvres, wedding cake, and champagne punch. Hannah's mother had given us the choice of limiting the guest list or eliminating the champagne service. We gave up the champagne. We bought the cake at a local coffeehouse, now defunct, where one of the bakers had trained at the fanciest bakery in San Francisco. It cost $100, a good price for a good cake. Different layers were different flavors, an innovation back then. They baked a sample cake for free; Hannah had them write "Happy Birthday, Mom," and used it for her mother's birthday.

The reception was held at the Marines Memorial Club. My father had been a career officer in the Marine Corps and a charter member of the club; Meg used his dress saber to cut her cake, just as Hannah had used her grandfather's military sword to cut hers. Hannah's parents also were members of the club; her father had been an army officer.

My sister's church wedding and backyard reception two years prior had cost $1,000. Ours cost $2,000, and we did not feel that it was outrageous. That $2,000 would be about $11,300 now, due to inflation. On the other hand, the price of duplicating our wedding would now cost more than $55,000.

For $2,000 we were able to get the wedding we wanted. We like to dress up, put on a big show, and have a party. And even the local vendors and the staffs of the cathedral and the Marines Memorial Club seemed to have a good time. And the best part? We've had almost forty-four years of a great marriage as well.

ରେଚ୍ଚ

What My Parents' 1974 Wedding Would Cost in 2020

We all know how inflation works. In fact, it's so predictable that many of us get cost-of-living increases in our wages to keep pace with it. But you know what almost nobody understands? Wedding inflation. Wedding inflation has run rampant over the past few decades, and we've certainly never gotten a cost-of-living increase for it. As a professional observer of the wedding industry, I've talked about wedding inflation everywhere from NPR to the *Atlantic*. But until a few years ago, I'd never gotten a chance to actually prove my case. Then in 2017, BuzzFeed asked me if I'd do a deep dive into my parents' wedding budget to see what it would cost to re-create it forty years later—and to illustrate what wedding inflation really looks like. My dad loved my mom, loved their wedding, and really, *really* loved numbers. Which meant that I had access to their line-by-line wedding budget, which he'd kept in his head for forty years. As a result, I was able to do a one-to-one comparison of their wedding costs in 1974 and what it would cost to re-create that wedding right now.

When you're in the middle of planning a wedding, the rising costs of weddings and expanded expectations around them get attributed to lavish tastes and poor decision making on behalf of you and your partner. So being able to show your math on wedding inflation is really helpful when you have to explain to your parents why the *hell* your wedding costs what it does. That article went on to garner well over a million views, but I never felt like it showed the full truth about wedding inflation. We'd tried so hard to not be hyperbolic, and we'd shaved off some of the costs of what it would cost to re-create their wedding today. So for this edition, we re-researched the whole project and got numbers that were as accurate as possible. And while my parents' wedding venue remains one of the most affordable places in San Francisco to get married . . . well . . . one quote to re-create their wedding cake came in at $12,000. No joke.

The problem is it's really hard to explain why things are *so* expensive in weddings, when often the answer is . . . they just are. But after a bunch of undercover phone calls to see what my parents' wedding would cost in 2020, I can tell you exactly how weddings are more expensive . . . and offer a few guesses as to why.

My Parents' Wedding:
> Total 1974 cost: $2,095
> What it should cost in 2020 dollars based on regular inflation: $11,316

The ceremony: My parents got married at Grace Cathedral in San Francisco. They weren't members of the congregation, but they were able to snag the membership discount in exchange for a kneeler, needlepointed by my grandmother. (Totally how weddings work now, right? Right . . .)
> 1974 cost: $250
> What it should cost in 2020 dollars: $1,320
> What it actually costs in 2020: $8,650
> Increase: 555 percent

Invitations: My parents sent out three hundred engraved wedding invitations, which is the most traditional, formal, and expensive method you can choose.
> 1974 cost: $250
> What it should cost in 2020 dollars: $1,573
> What it actually costs in 2020: $3,490
> Increase: 122 percent

Flowers: The wedding took place three days after Christmas, so for the ceremony they used the flowers that were still up from the holidays—which means their floral needs were relatively small: one bridal bouquet, three bridesmaid bouquets, flowers for the flower girl, and two arrangements for the cake table at the reception with chrysanthemum and ivy. Had they wanted decorations for the church? Grace Cathedral currently has an "approved florist list," and the first one I clicked on had a minimum order of $8,000.

And in case you thought you'd be thrifty and reuse some of your ceremony decor at the reception? *Nope*; not allowed. Flowers brought into the church for decoration must be donated to the church after the wedding. Which might seem reasonable if those altar flowers didn't cost *$8,000 at minimum.*

As it stands, personal flowers can come from anywhere, so we sent some photos of my parents' bouquets to our friendly local florist for a quote (though many florists in San Francisco these days don't get out of bed for less than $4,000, so in reality you may end up with more flowers than my parents had . . . and a much higher bill.)

> 1974 cost: $50
>
> What it should cost in 2020 dollars: $264
>
> What it actually costs in 2020: $1,400
>
> Increase: 430 percent

Photography: My parents met their (very experienced) photographer when he shot my aunt's wedding. He had subsequently raised his rates but was willing to honor the old price . . . a whopping $50. And while with enough elbow grease (or Craigslist skills) you can find photographers at almost any rate these days, most professional photographers working in San Francisco will be priced at $3,500 or above—and that's on the conservative side. Everyone we spoke to said a formal church ceremony with three hundred guests would require at least eight hours and two photographers, so that would be at least $4,000.

> 1974 cost: $50
>
> What it should cost in 2020 dollars: $264
>
> What it actually costs in 2020: $4,000
>
> Increase: 1,415 percent

Bridal attire: Getting married in December meant my mom was able to get a nice wedding dress from the premier department store of the time during a half-off sale the previous spring. Recently (and blessedly), we've had an explosion of retailers offering more reasonably priced wedding dresses and accessories (both in store and online), so this was one line item where modernity worked in our favor.

> 1974 cost: $195
>
> What it should cost in 2020 dollars: $1,030
>
> What it actually costs in 2020: $1,250
>
> Increase: 21 percent

Cake: My parents' cake was ridiculous. Wedding cakes were bigger back in the day. And my parents got it into their heads that they wanted to serve birthday cake–size slices of cake, not teeny wedding cake slices. For three hundred people. There was . . . a lot of leftover cake.

In 2020? Of the handful of bakers we called for quotes, most of them didn't even offer a cake that big anymore (they recommended a smaller tiered cake to cut, supplemented with sheet cakes). But there were two vendors who were willing to indulge us with a quote for the huge cake, and they gave us two very different prices: one for $12,000 and the other for $5,400. We decided to opt for the simpler design and lower price.

> 1974 cost: $100
>
> What it should cost in 2020 dollars: $528
>
> What it actually costs in 2020: $5,400
>
> Increase: 923 percent

Reception and catering: In 2020 my parents would have had one of the cheapest options offered by the Marines Memorial Club: an afternoon lunch package for $80 per person. I called them up to see if it was possible to forgo the included open bar for a similar champagne punch setup, but they don't really do that anymore. But all in all? Getting the same package they got in 1974 would cost $31,248 today, including taxes and tip for all three hundred people. This still makes it one of the best deals in San Francisco.

> 1974 cost: $1,200
> What it should cost in 2020 dollars: $6,337
> What it actually costs in 2020: $31,248
> Increase: 393 percent

So for their entire wedding, we're looking at . . .

> Total 1974 cost: $2,095
> What it should cost in 2020 dollars: $11,316
> What it actually costs in 2020: $55,438
> Increase: 390 percent

You read that right. That is almost a 400 percent increase in what it would cost to throw my parents' wedding. Why? It's kind of a chicken-and-egg thing. Sometime between 1974 and today, people realized that weddings weren't necessarily a side business. And now there's a whole industry around weddings. An industry that, as Rebecca Mead writes in *One Perfect Day: The Selling of the American Wedding*, has been "assiduous in working to establish the trappings of the lavish formal wedding as if they were compulsory rather than optional." Most wedding vendors are also small-business owners who are charging for the increase in time, attention, and *perfection* that couples and their parents have come to expect (not to mention the fact that living and working in San Francisco is decidedly more expensive than it was in 1974).

Expectations around weddings are much higher than they used to be, and everything is now considered mandatory in order to have a "real wedding." Which you already know if you've ever heard someone say, "Well, it's not a wedding if you don't [serve three kinds of steak/hire a professional photographer for fourteen hours/wear crystal-studded stilettos]." And the phenomenon of higher expectations feeds into higher costs, which feeds into even higher expectations, and the whole thing just snowballs until you feel gaslit by both the wedding industry and your family and say, "Forget it. Let's elope."

So the next time someone suggests that they know how to plan your wedding better than you do, tell them you'd gladly take them up on their offer to be your wedding planner. After all, wedding planners aren't cheap these days.

What Is Tradition Anyway?

Tradition is a very slippery thing. It's possible to argue that home weddings are traditional, or jumping over the broom is traditional, or boozy flapper weddings are traditional, or weddings in social halls with punch and cake are traditional. It's a lot harder to argue that unity candles and wedding favors are traditional, but that doesn't stop people from trying. If something is done often enough, the wedding industry is able to convince us that it's actual tradition, with an actual historical connection, and that we'd be insulting our mothers and our grandmothers if we didn't do it (even if they'd never heard of it and would have laughed at it if they had).

Just for fun, let's come up with a list of things that don't have a long historical tradition of any sort: the bridal bouquet (emerged around the turn of the century, before which women held prayer books or handkerchiefs), the once-worn formal white dress (became popular in the early to mid-twentieth century thanks to a serious marketing effort), the catered reception (came into vogue in the 1950s), and the unity candle (invented in the 1970s as part of a soap-opera script). And we could go on and on and on.

The real key is discovering what tradition means to you and to your family. While women have not been getting married in churches for time immemorial, maybe your mother and your grandmother got married in a church, and perhaps you want to follow in their footsteps. If a tradition means something to you or to the people you love, you should pay attention to it. But if it doesn't, ignore it. Unless your religion requires it, it's not mandatory that you get married in a church, nor is it particularly historical. You're not thumbing your nose at the order of things if you don't have all of the frills of a church wedding (an aisle runner, programs, a wedding party, and so on). Tradition is malleable and varied, and what's important is that you make it yours.

> A sk yourself: Whose tradition is this anyway? I consider tradition something that should provide nourishment and challenge us on emotional and spiritual levels; it is a place where we can belong and can ask our questions.
>
> —Clare Adama, a theologian who married in Edinburgh

Etiquette Isn't About Spending Money

Not only is tradition not quite what you've been led to believe, but etiquette is also a lot less demanding than expected. And there is a distinct difference between the dictates of the wedding industry and actual etiquette. There are many lovely people in the wedding industry, but when those people have a financial interest in your impending nuptials, it's helpful to take their advice with a grain of salt. "Hmm," one might say, "if I follow this advice, will it involve me spending more money? Yes? Well, then does this sound like real tradition, or the kind someone made up?" Because the wedding industry can be self-serving. When a photographer tells you that the best way to afford an expensive photographer is to cut your guest list because guests are expensive, it's appropriate to raise an eyebrow. When a bridal magazine tells you that it's mandatory to purchase expensive invitations, again, take a pause.

But the trouble is that faux tradition is more insidious than we even suspect. The catered reception? Not historical at all. So when books and magazines instruct you that it's more proper to have your wedding reception dinner served by waiters in black tie than to have it served buffet style, it can be tricky to remember that every single thing about that sentiment is made up. Even in your parents' day, most people didn't serve a full wedding meal, so etiquette has nothing to say about how this newly mandated meal *should* be served.

What Is Etiquette Anyway, and Is It Stuffy?

Which brings us to etiquette itself: What is it, and how much should you pay attention to it?

Let's define etiquette this way: It is about making sure that other people's feelings are taken into consideration. It's about graciousness. Think of it as a speed bump on the road to self-absorbed wedding hell. One of the ways to be kind to those around us is to treat our shared cultural history with a healthy sense of respect. This doesn't mean that we have to do everything the way it has "always been done" (since, as we've discussed, most things haven't been done that way for very long in the first place). It's about understanding where your granny is coming from and making allowances for her if you're doing something she'll find disorienting.

Etiquette is not something to be scared of. It's on the side of simplicity and common sense. It is decidedly not on the side of the "Spend more! Personalize it! Make it yours!" wedding culture, and anyone who leads you to believe that is lying.

ℓℓℓℓ

The Registry: It's Not Actually for You

If you're like me, wrapping your mind around the registry might be hard. There is part of your brain that screams "We're engaged! Free stuff! Hooray!" and part of your brain that wonders why finding a life partner entitles you to plates, especially when you already have plates. Here is what it took me a long time to figure out: The registry is not for you. In fact, the registry has almost nothing to do with your wedding. Your registry is for your guests and for your marriage.

When guests go to a wedding, they want a way to participate. They don't just want to participate in the party (because to do that, they can just get drunk and do the conga line). They want to find a way to show their support for your marriage. Your wedding day is your first day together as a formal family unit in the eyes of society, and all of the people gathered around with fierce hopes and dreams for you understand that. They know that getting married is easy, but building a life together is hard. They want to support you in the hard part.

The registry is like a barn raising. It gives your guests a time-honored way to tell you that they are with you for the long haul. When you get gifts of sturdy stoneware plates to replace the chipped thrift-store dishes in your cupboards, your loved ones are not being materialistic. They're tangibly showing their love to you through plates that will make it through fights, and moves, and (possibly) kids. They want to show their love for you with plates that you'll take with you to the retirement home.

So no matter what decisions you make about your registry, remember this: You're not getting gifts and cash because you somehow deserve it. You're getting gifts and cash because people are showing their love. The registry isn't about the wedding, and it isn't about you. It's about letting your friends and loved ones build a home for you. It's about letting them love you.

ℓℓℓℓ

Simplicity Rules

Before we dive into all-the-things-you've-been-told-are-proper-but-really-are-nonsense, here are some issues of etiquette that you really should pay attention to (even if you haven't been hearing much about these particular rules):

- **On your wedding day, you are hosting your loved ones.** Wedding literature seems bent on convincing us that the wedding day is all about *you*. And it is, sort of. You are the one getting married. But whenever you are hosting a party for a lot of your friends and loved ones, one of your primary responsibilities is making sure those people are taken care of. So when making etiquette decisions, try to keep your guests firmly in mind. Feed your guests on time. Don't force them to wear outfits that match your color scheme. Thank them for attending. Don't boss them around. Treat them like they are people you love and show them that you are honored to have them spending an important day with you. If you do this, I will join etiquette in giving you a delighted thumbs-up.

- **Your wedding day should be a reflection of your life as it's lived.** No money for gold-plated swans in your day-to-day life? Well, lucky enough, that means you're off the hook for providing gold-plated swans for your wedding reception (even if the lack of such swans is going to hurt your aunt Mindy's feelings). Anyone who tries to make you feel guilty about not having a lavish wedding is, in fact, acting in very poor taste.

- **Your wedding day should reflect your loved ones as they are.** Your mom doesn't need to go on a diet to look like someone she's not on your wedding day. Your long-estranged father shouldn't walk you down the aisle. You don't need wedding parties in matching sizes or genders. Etiquette is, after all, about taking the emotions of those you love into consideration, not about following a bunch of made-up rules that mindlessly hurt people's feelings.

> **You are allowed to leave out traditions.** There is no rule that you have to collect every wedding tradition that's ever been created and try to cram it into a few hours on your wedding day. If a tradition doesn't mean something to you, you're allowed to let it go. You're not allowed to rub people's faces in the fact that you are the more evolved person and therefore are not doing things that they did at their wedding. That's unkind. But you are allowed to quietly go about creating a ritual that works for you and not spend a minute worrying that you're doing something improper.

> **Your wedding is not a show.** There is a lot of material out there that would lead you to believe that your wedding is best viewed as a production that should be geared for the maximum entertainment of your guests. It's not, and most of your guests know better. Your wedding consists of a ceremony, where you make hugely emotional vows, followed by a party to celebrate that commitment, and that's more than enough. It doesn't need to be gussied up with paper goods and lighting and fancy dresses. It can be, but those things are for fun's sake, not for etiquette's sake.

Okay, Fine, Details on Wedding Etiquette

All right, all right. I gave you the overarching general principles of wedding etiquette, but you have specific questions, and most of the advice out there seems regressive at best. To be clear, wedding etiquette shouldn't involve throwing your feminist/progressive/millennial values to the curb. Instead, it should give you a way to live out those values—while still trying to make your parents, grandparents, and friends feel loved and included.

After ten years in the industry, two wedding books, and thousands upon thousands of hours of research, I feel comfortable helping you throw some awful rules out the window, while also telling you which rules you're probably stuck with.

What's the Deal with Engagement Parties?

Engagement parties are 100 percent optional, but if you decide to have one, they can be as formal or informal as you'd like. Party at a bar? Fine. Family member wants to throw you a black-tie party at a restaurant? As long as they're willing to pay, sure!

Who Hosts the Shower, and Do We Have to Have One?

Once upon a time, the wedding etiquette rule was that showers couldn't be hosted by family members because it looked too "gift grabby." That rule is thankfully out the window. Anyone can host your shower! If a member of the wedding party, friend, or family member offers to host a prewedding shower, say yes if you want to. But word to the wise: there is such a thing as too many showers. If you have offers for showers from both sides of the family, your wedding party, and your work, consider consolidating before you burn out.

Who Pays for What?

Back in the day, the bride's family paid for basically everything because . . . women were considered financial burdens, passed from one male to another. If you weren't offering a dowry, you could at least offer a party that cost as much as a dowry. Since nobody is unburdening themselves of an economic liability these days (and you might not even be a mixed-gender couple), payment should be split in a way that makes financial sense for everyone involved.

Do I Send Invites to People I Know Can't Attend?

If you love someone, and really wish they could be at your wedding, send them an invite. Your guests are adults, and they can and will say no if attending isn't practical for them. But it's an honor to be invited to someone's wedding. Don't take that away from someone just because you know they're not going to be able to make it.

Who Gets a Plus-One?

If your people are married or in a long-term relationship, it's required by wedding etiquette—yes, required—to invite their partner. It's kind to offer single guests the ability to bring a date, and it increases the odds that they'll attend. (Social anxiety is real.) But if you can't afford—or really don't want—those extra guests, the "and guest" invitation is never required.

Do I Have to Invite All My Cousins/Coworkers?

Nope! But it is helpful to set general rules, so feelings are not hurt. Maybe all first cousins are in, but second cousins are out. Maybe co-workers on your direct team are in, but your extended department is out. (Besties are obviously an exception to any rule.)

Do We Have to Send Paper Invites to Be Taken Seriously?

Short answer: No.

Long answer: If you want your great-grandmother to attend, you probably need to send her a paper invitation (or call her). That's not about wedding etiquette; it's about practicality. But you're in luck, because almost all e-invitation services give you the option of sending out matching paper invitations to selected guests. Figure out which of your guests are really not plugged in and send them something in the mail.

Can We Have an "Experience" Registry?

You sure can. But the bottom line is, some people will get you physical presents because that's just how they do things. And that's okay. A present is just that: a present. It's not something you deserve or can expect. In short: ask for what you want; be happy with what you get.

Can We Ask for Cash?

"Can I ask for cash?" and "Will I get cash?" are somewhat different questions, so let's break it down. Yes, you can ask for cash. But fair warning: depending on your crowd, there may be people who don't like it. That said, if you quietly put out the word that you'd prefer cash because you're saving for a particular thing (moms and best friends are great for broadcasting this message, by the way), and provide only a minimal registry, you may well get a lot of cash, if only because it's easier.

Does Wedding Etiquette Require That Guests Bring a Gift?

Required is a strong word there, grasshopper. It's recommended that guests bring a wedding gift, but I'm pretty sure you'd rather have them there than have a toaster. Also, the idea that gifts need to cover the cost of the meal is false. Make sure you have $10 and $20 items on your registry for the broke folks.

Is XYZ Thing I'm Doing Gift Grabby?

NO. No, no, no. Unless you're doing it to actually make a play for extra presents, in which case, yes.

Do We Have to Send Thank-You Notes?

Short answer: Yes.

Long answer: If someone brought a gift to your wedding, they need to be thanked. If that someone is under thirty and casual in nature, thank them however you see fit. Text? Snapchat? Instagram tag? If that's how the two of you comfortably communicate, it's fine to express your genuinely felt gratitude that way. However, if your gift giver is over thirty, you probably need to send a card on paper with an actual stamp, as etiquette has always required. I know: OLDS. But hey, you will be an old one day soon, just like the rest of us, so be kind.

How Long Do We Have to Send Thank-You Notes?

Technically, you have a year. Realistically, you probably should send them within two or three months.

Reclaiming Traditions

Dealing with (Well-Meaning?) Advice

People like to use words like *etiquette* and *tradition* to get you to fulfill their vision of what your wedding should be. When people are trying to push you around, correct information, casually mentioned, can do wonders. "Actually," you say, "for most of the history of the United States, people got married at home. So really I'm trying to embrace something traditional in a way that's meaningful to me."

People also use the word *etiquette* out of fear. "But we have to do it this way" can be code for "I'm afraid my friends will judge me if we don't." If the person who's afraid of judgment is someone you love (mothers are particularly prone to the Wedding Judgment Fear), the best thing you can do is talk things out with them and find out what their real reasons are for insisting on XYZ wedding tradition. Information might help, but what's really going to fix it is getting to the root of what she's afraid of and empowering her with a little "f*ck 'em if they don't like the chairs" philosophy. Because, yes, sometimes moms need to be reminded that they are allowed to not care what other people think, too.

Remember, planning a wedding is the first step you will take as part of the process of creating a new family in the eyes of your community. Part of the (sometimes painful) process of owning your new role is learning to stand up to people. Graciously. When people push you around, inform them of what you're doing and why. Or change the subject. Your wedding is your business, and etiquette holds no truck with bullying.

> **P**eople have opinions about everything, and there were times when I cried because of thoughtless things that were said about decisions we were making: to not have a wedding party, to have very unique rings, to have a piñata and fire truck exit, to get ready together, etc. But I am so happy for each choice we made that went against the grain but felt like us.
>
> —Max Devore Williams, who married her husband in a green velvet dress on the coast of Northern California

Tradition Is Not a Bad Word

Tradition is what you make of it. When you decide to get married, you are, in a sense, choosing to side with tradition. When we started planning our wedding, we asked my parents if they wanted veto power on any of our decisions, and they shrugged it off. My dad explained, "First, we trust your judgment. Second, with weddings, tradition always wins, because getting married is, in its very essence, traditional. So make whatever choices you want. They'll be traditional enough."

And for me, this is the essence of tradition—a way to sort through a long history of ritual and create something that's meaningful to you. Clare Adama, a theologian who got married in Edinburgh, Scotland, wisely advised, "The Latin origin of tradition, 'traditio,' means not only to hand on but to hand over, and the meanings of practices such as those within weddings are not rigid, but given on to us to value and interpret in our own contexts." Weddings provide us a wonderful opportunity to sit down and discuss who we are and what we believe with our partners. We do ourselves a great disservice when we allow tradition to be the things that we are sold instead of the things that have meaning in our hearts. Embrace the aspects of wedding rituals that have meaning to you, and let the rest go. Know that no matter what you choose, you'll be standing on the shoulders of many people who have gone before you.

And as for etiquette, well, if you're being kind and thoughtful, you're probably doing just fine. Be sure to raise an eyebrow at anyone who tells you otherwise.

WEDDING HOMEWORK

- Planning a wedding is a great excuse to get your friends and loved ones to tell you the unvarnished stories of their own weddings, so go forth and ask all your favorite family members to tell you all about their weddings. (You'll want these stories later. My dad died a year before the publication of the second edition of this book, and I am so glad that I have his version of my parents' wedding story down in print.) Ask family members what they loved about their wedding. Ask them what went right. Ask them what went wrong.
- Ask your family members what their wedding cost. If they're open to it, figure out together what it would cost in inflation-adjusted dollars and what it would cost to throw the same wedding now.
- Sit down with your partner and discuss what traditions are important to each of you (and why) and decide what you want to meaningfully incorporate into your wedding, and what you want to throw in the trash. As always, I suggest that you write two lists and then write one comprehensive list with everything you want to include in your wedding.
- Have the same conversation about etiquette. How were you each raised? What internalized rules do you have about what constitutes polite behavior? Do they mesh? Do they not? Discuss how this might influence your life together, beyond your wedding day.
- Mantra when you're overwhelmed by all the "shoulds": "Our wedding is not a show."

In the Party-Planning Trenches

ℰ—— Beyond the Spreadsheets ——৲৩

- ⁊ Wedding planning is not going to change your fundamental nature, so own it. This is a great opportunity to practice self-acceptance and self-love. Focus on what you're good at and forget (or hire people to help with) the rest.
- ⁊ When making wedding decisions, remember that the best is the enemy of the good. Lots of good-enough decisions can make something pretty great, so just make the decision already.
- ⁊ Hire vendors you like and trust. You'll work closely with them, and it's not worth sacrificing sanity for style.
- ⁊ Your wedding party is a way to honor important people in your life. So forget whatever you think the rules are and focus on what works for you and your loved ones.
- ⁊ Trust yourself. Choose things that will make you grin on your wedding day.

Oh! You Mean I Have to Plan This Thing?

Suddenly it hits. You're in the middle of planning your wedding. As it turns out, it's not exactly the easiest thing you've ever done. After looking at a lot of wedding magazines (so pretty) and going down the Pinterest rabbit hole (so addicting), it's deceptively easy to start thinking that planning a wedding is as simple as making a series of inspiration boards and picking pretty things. And while we *will* talk about picking pretty things, first let's formulate a method for surviving the harder parts of wedding planning: hiring vendors and signing contracts. Wedding planning is as much about decision making as it is about style.

Know Thyself and Be Thyself

To survive wedding planning sane, you need to find a way to embrace your basic nature. Kristina Loring, who threw a RuPaul-inspired celebration with her wife on a small island near their hometown of Portland, Maine, told me, "As it turned out, things I don't love doing at work are the same things I didn't want to do for my wedding. I faced reality, and we hired a planner to help with those things. Just as being married isn't going to suddenly transform everything in your relationship, weddings aren't going to suddenly change the type of person you are." The sooner you own up to this, the better off you'll be.

You're a pretty fantastic person just the way you are (that's why someone is committing to you for life). Take a second to think about what you're good at and what is not your bag. When you're throwing a party in your regular life, what are your strengths and weaknesses? What parts are you brilliant at? The food? Decorating? Selecting the right group of people? Throwing an informal party together quickly? What parts are you terrible at? I'm good at motivating people to come to our parties, and my husband is excellent at serving the right food and drink, but we're both a little loosey-goosey with budgeting. When we're throwing a party, we come up with an idea that seems affordable and buy as we go. We inevitably end up realizing the party cost a little more than we intended . . . but was even more fun than we'd hoped. Given this, it is no great surprise that our wedding had great people and great food, but our budget "tracker" was a Post-it. (Do as I say, not as I do.) Think of your wedding as a dolled-up version of the parties you normally throw. It will give you permission to play and get fancy but will help you to set realistic expectations.

This is also a great time to examine where you need help. If you're terrible at organization (which we'll discuss in greater depth in Chapter 8) and are having a big wedding, now might be the time to ask a friend to help or to hire a wedding planner. (Trust me, a big wedding is a big undertaking. Don't lie to yourself on that front.) If you're terrible at cooking, for goodness' sake, hire a caterer. The bottom line is, we can't always do it all, and we don't need to.

Edit, Edit, Edit

Here is the deep, dark secret of wedding planning: not everything matters. Trying to do everything will turn you into a crazy person. Brandi Hassouna, who married in a friend's home in Los Angeles, put it this way: "Just the thought of most of the details I initially wanted left me wrung out. I just couldn't do it. My architect fiancé stepped in when he saw me slowly tearing my hair out and suggested we do what all creatives do, edit edit edit . . . and then edit a bit more. The house became the color palette. We added a few lanterns with battery-powered LEDs, some pom-poms, a few flower arrangements, and ta-da, the house was ready for a party." Wedding planning has a way of making every small detail seem important, but you can't split your focus between one hundred details. So take a moment to refocus yourself. Go back to the list you made in Chapter 1, look at what you really care about, and allow that to shape which details you will focus on. You might need chairs, but unless you put it on the high-priority list when you started planning, you don't have to care about what they look like.

The Gut Check

Modern wedding planning has a way of immobilizing you, making decisions impossible. Because of the way the human brain works, the more choices we have, the more we are both frozen with indecision and ultimately unhappy with our choice. We're terrified that we'll choose incorrectly.

Remember, each choice gets you a step closer to getting married, and nothing is a life-or-death decision, no matter how it feels. I made my best wedding decisions the week before the wedding because I didn't have time to dither. I would look at two options, give myself five seconds to think about which one seemed best for us, and go with it. This sort of rapid-fire gut check is a profoundly helpful way to approach the million decisions that you need to make during wedding planning. Sure, your gut might not always be right, but in the end the little decisions are not going to matter much anyway, so you might as well not waste tons of emotional energy making them. That said, Christen Karle Muir, who married in an old Catholic church in a coastal Northern California town, told me, "Trust your gut, yes, but know that it is okay if your gut has no idea. The most important thing is being okay with your decision, no matter what, after the fact." Make choices that you can live with and then move on. Hopefully, you've picked a good partner to marry, and the rest of your choices will become details.

The Best Is the Enemy of the Good

When it comes to making individual wedding decisions, quote Voltaire: "The best is the enemy of the good." Or in other words, good is sometimes good enough, and our endless quest for perfection often ends with us sacrificing good options while we look for the elusive "best" option. If we wait and wait to pick a wedding vendor because we're not sure the ones we have found are quite right, all of the good vendors might end up booked before we bite the bullet. So gather your nerve and choose. I can guarantee you that you won't make perfect choices. But I can also guarantee that if you try to make choices that feel right to you, and make you happy, they will usually be good enough. And the sum of lots of things that are good enough is actually pretty great.

More Decisions (Yes, They Keep Coming)

Now that we've discussed some less crazy ways to make decisions (not everything matters, the best is the enemy of the good, just choose already), let's talk about some of the bigger decisions you are making. Hiring vendors and signing contracts is something you want to go into with your head screwed on straight because you should be fond of anyone you're paying a small pile of money. Then there are the personal choices, like deciding if you want a wedding party, picking your wedding party, and making peace with the wedding party you've got. And finally, you'll need to make decisions about all of those pesky wedding-related parties. Do you need them? (No.) Do you want them? (Maybe.) Can you make them into something that makes sense for you? (Yes.)

Hiring Vendors

When it comes to making choices, some of the most expensive decisions involve hiring your wedding vendors. Right up front, I want to free you from the burden of doing endless research in the quest to hire perfect wedding vendors (there are no perfect vendors). Instead, you should focus your vendor search on finding people you personally mesh with. In five years, the wedding photography trends will have changed, but you'll still have memories of the photographer who followed you everywhere on your wedding day, and you want those memories to be genuinely happy, not hilariously horrifying.

This is a good time to remind you why your vendor choices matter. Your photographer, should you choose to have one, will be following you around like your personal paparazzo (lying on the ground literally underneath you to get a shot during your first dance). Your venue and caterer will be in charge of making sure things go smoothly (that the doors are unlocked and that the tables and food are set up). And your officiant will take on the monumental task of binding you to another person for life (hopefully with a minimum of awkward jokes and banter). And while there is no perfect, there is definitely . . . bad. So listen to your gut when you're choosing whom to hire. The officiant who makes slightly sexist jokes during your interview? Probably not the ideal candidate. The wedding photographer the Internet says is a must-hire, but who doesn't promptly return your calls and makes you feel not-cool-enough over tea? Skip 'em.

When you can, find people whose philosophy you agree with and who make you laugh. When you can't, find people who seem relatively unobjectionable and don't raise any red flags. And feel free to be very clear about expressing your needs and wants. We did not want photographers in our face during our religious service, nor did we want them bossing our guests around during the reception (we'd seen both happen at other weddings). Being really explicit about this in vendor interviews helped us find exactly the right photographers to work with. At the end of the day, beautiful images are great, but a wedding photographer who makes you feel gorgeous and happy while following you around on your wedding day is probably better.

Contracts

Hiring wedding vendors isn't just about finding someone you personally mesh with; it's also about signing a legally binding contract. While oral contracts can often be enforced when there is a problem, you don't need that headache. Get it in writing. Make sure you have a contract with all of your wedding vendors, even if (perhaps especially if) they are a friend of a friend. Just because you get along with the person you hired doesn't mean that you shouldn't both be protected in case something goes awry. Your contract should stipulate the deposit needed to secure your date and when your remaining payments are due. It should lay out what happens if one of you is unable to fulfill the contract, and it should offer you protections if the contract is not fulfilled up to the standards stated. Perhaps most important, you should feel comfortable negotiating respectfully with your vendors if their standard contract has a clause that makes you uncomfortable. Contracts are a starting point for discussion, not the ending point. Anything that makes you uneasy should be discussed before the contract is signed.

ℓℓℓℓ

It's a Nice Day for a Non-White Wedding

By Jareesa Tucker McClure

Wedding planning is a daunting endeavor for almost every couple, but for people of color it can be even more fraught and, frankly, anxiety inducing. With the lack of diversity in mainstream wedding media, you can feel like a bit of a unicorn. A lot of traditional spaces are overwhelmingly White, but you can find inspiration, resources, and support from people of color if you know where to look and whom to talk to.

Look to Other Couples for Inspiration. The traditional wedding-industrial complex has been slow to embrace and feature brides of color, whether it's in blogs, magazines, or other resources. So when looking for inspiration, your best bet is to turn to other couples. Thanks to social media, it's easier to find photos and other resources highlighting both brides of color and vendors of color. Try using resources like Instagram and Pinterest to find other like-minded brides for inspiration.

⚬ Hashtags and keywords are your friend. My first search on Instagram was #blackbride, and it led me down an amazing rabbit hole of content that I wasn't otherwise seeing. Try searching terms that describe who you are—#bridesofcolor,

(continues)

#asianbride, #muslimbride, etc. Instagram allows you to follow hashtags, so inspiration can be delivered directly to your news feed.

⚘ Seek out wedding publications that speak exclusively to your identity. For example, you can do a Google search for "Black bridal magazine" and see what pops up. If you're not sure where to find certain publications, search Pinterest for specific traditions (e.g., jumping the broom), as those photos often lead you to published weddings that feature the kind of folks you're looking for.

Embrace Your Cultural Traditions. Many brides of color want to plan a wedding day that incorporates some part of their cultural heritage. Here are some ways to find traditions that are meaningful to you and ideas on how to incorporate them:

⚘ Our families and community elders are a great resource of cultural traditions, including some you may not be aware of. In talking to your grandmother, you may learn that your family has jumped the same wedding broom for generations. Maybe there's a special accessory that all the women in your family wear. Maybe there is a beloved tradition you've never heard of. You won't know until you ask (and chances are your grandmother will be so thrilled that you did).

⚘ Are there specific rituals or activities that tie into your culture? For me, it was jumping the broom. Many Black Americans who are descended from slaves choose to jump the broom at the end of their ceremonies to acknowledge their ancestors who were unable to legally wed.

⚘ If you're able, share some context with your guests on your traditions and why they are performed. A great place to do this is in the wedding program, or you could have your officiant do a quick explanation.

Find Vendors Who Acknowledge That You're a Person of Color. It's a fact that people of color have different needs, and that's okay. It's important to find vendors who are respectful, see you as a person, and are able to provide the services you need. For me, this came into play when selecting our photographer, as well as my hair and makeup artists. As a Black woman marrying a Black man, finding a photographer who understood how to properly light and photograph darker skin was crucial. Similarly, I wanted beauty professionals who had experience working with darker-skinned women and natural hair textures. No vendor should make you feel that your concerns or needs are not valid, and if they do, keep looking! If you're not sure a wedding vendor will be a good fit for your wedding, here are some ways to vet them before you sign that contract:

- ⚘ Ask to see examples of their work that feature people of color. This is especially important for vendors like your photographer or your makeup artist. It's really important to verify that they have the tools and skills to provide you with great service.
- ⚘ Do a test run, if you can. If you're trying out a photographer, see if you can do an engagement session and simulate different lighting situations. Everyone can shoot outside with natural lighting, but how do they do indoors in candlelight?
- ⚘ Get referrals! Social media and your friend networks are great for this. Ask for recommendations for great vendors who have worked with other people of color. Recently married couples are very eager to share both the vendors they loved and the vendors that they regretted, so don't hesitate to ask the questions and get names.

ℓℓℓℓ

Your Wedding Party—Creating #SquadGoals

For many of us, a major wedding planning decision is figuring out what our wedding party should look like. On the surface, it seems like picking bridesmaids and groomsmen should be easy, but in reality, it's often not. First, and most fundamentally, the wedding party is a way to honor important people in your lives. These people should be a reflection of your life as it's lived, not an attempt to style your life so that it looks like a magazine picture.

The Fundamentals:

- ⇝ You don't need the exact same number of attendants as your partner.
- ⇝ Attendants do not need to be split along gender lines (your best guy friend can and should stand up for you).
- ⇝ Your attendants do not have to wear matching outfits.
- ⇝ You do not have to give your attendants expensive gifts. If you want to give them something, give them a framed picture of you both on your wedding day and a heartfelt letter. Friendship is free; don't let anyone convince you otherwise.

And There's More:

- ⇝ Your attendants aren't required to stand up at your ceremony. You can find other ways to honor them (readings, songs, symbolic religious duties).
- ⇝ You don't need a formal wedding party.
- ⇝ You don't have to have a wedding party at all.

Here Is the Real Truth

For most of us, the wedding party isn't completely painless. Many of us don't have people willing to drop all of their plans and fly across the country to throw us bridal showers, or five model-thin friends that look good in eggshell blue, or four girls we've been best friends with since we were five. Maybe we don't even *have* piles of best friends. And that's fine. The point is to find a way to honor people we love and to have people around us on our wedding day who make us feel supported. Maybe you want a traditional wedding party in all matching dresses. Maybe you just want a group of people who love you and support you to take your phone calls when you're freaking out about your wedding. Just know that there is no one way to do things and that wedding parties are always a little imperfect, just like friendships.

The Wedding Party Bill of Rights

When you ask someone to be in your wedding party, it's easy to start thinking that normal rules don't apply. You're getting married, after all, and chances are that you're extremely excited about this huge party being thrown in your honor. It's easy to get sucked into thinking that the wedding is as important to everyone else as it is to you and throw common sense out the window. But before you do, some thoughts:

- ⸎ People in your life are not going to change their fundamental personalities just because they are in your wedding party. If your best friend is a disorganized mess, expect that to continue when she's your maid of honor.
- ⸎ Keep your loved ones' real-life budgets in mind. If you're asking your people to wear expensive dresses, consider offering to pay for them.
- ⸎ Think about overall cost. Your wedding party isn't just paying for their outfits. They are also paying for their travel, your gifts, and maybe bridal shower or bachelorette party expenses as well. Be thoughtful about what you ask from them financially and remember to show your gratitude.
- ⸎ Showers and bachelorette parties are optional. If someone offers to throw you a shower, thank them. If you throw yourself a bachelorette party, remember the time and energy people are putting into coming, and thank them again. Most important, if some of your wedding party can't attend these events, be understanding. (I swear, they still love you!)
- ⸎ Ask their opinions. Wedding Land is not always the most rational place to be. So, if you're convinced that the lime-green fluffy ball gowns are the best bridesmaid dresses ever, and your ladies are less convinced, listen to them. If they try to talk you off a stress ledge, keep listening.

(continues)

- Remember the purpose of your wedding party. They are there to hold your hand when you're stressed, support you on your wedding day, and stand up for you and your marriage for the rest of your life. The outfits they wear are just icing on the cake.

A note to wedding party members: Remember, your job is to make the couple's life easier (while still being your charming self). Getting married is stressful in ways that are sometimes hard to comprehend from the outside. Ask the couple how they're feeling and what you can do to support them. And if they still insist that the lime-green fluffy ball gown is stunning, suck it up and celebrate your ass off in that dress. That's what showing up for a friend means.

Parties, Showers, Bachelorettes, Oh My

As the modern wedding industry has expanded (and expanded and expanded), more and more parties have made it to the list of Things You Must Have in Order to Get Married. That list currently includes the engagement party, the wedding shower (or showers), the bachelor party, and the bachelorette party. Which is a whole lot of extra parties to worry about when you're dealing with planning one of the biggest parties of your life.

Should some of these parties happen to you, you should embrace them and enjoy them. But please don't think that these parties are (1) traditional and mandatory, (2) something your bridesmaids are required to throw for you, or (3) an indication of how much the people around you love you. In fact, these are optional parties that you should enjoy if they happen and not worry about if they don't. And no, you can't require people to throw them for you (though you can nicely ask for help, or even throw the parties for yourself, if they really matter to you).

And Yes, Wedding Style

When planning a wedding, decisions about how things are going to look tend to take up a lot of brain space. Wedding media like to focus on the pretty bits, and it's fun to get sucked into planning the little details. What kind of table numbers are you going to have? What style of wedding dress do you want? What is your color palette? Weddings are pretty. Pretty is fun. And the pretty stuff can be a good way to distract you from the harder parts of the process. So, if the details are enjoyable to you, by all means embrace this part of wedding planning.

But if at any point the pretty parts of wedding planning stop being fun and start making you crazy, take a deep breath and reassess. Michelle Edgemont, a wedding designer who got married in a public social hall in Pennsylvania, went through some serious wedding planning stress before she had a revelation: "I stopped reading anything that made me feel inferior, crazy, self-conscious, or dumb." When wedding aesthetics stop being a fun project and start being a maddening quest to keep up, it's time to take a step back.

The Details: How They Matter, How They Don't

Back in Chapter 1, I made you tack up the phrase "I will not remember what our wedding looked like; I will remember what it felt like" in a place where you could see it every day. While you should be thinking about that with every decision you make, you still probably need to make decisions about your wedding aesthetics. Nicole Kazee, who had a pig roast at her reception in a small resort town in Michigan, said, "You're going to have to make a million little decisions, regardless of whether you actually care or not, but the focus should be on choosing big things that will shape the spirit of it all—things that get you wildly, deeply excited." For example, before Anna Shapiro's interfaith wedding, she asked people to craft quilt squares that she sewed into the huppah they married under. In this way, the aesthetics became important because they allowed people to be included in the ritual of marriage. She said, "I was sure that on the actual day I would feel like an idiot for having put so much energy into unimportant details. But when I looked around this room full of most of the people that I love in this world, all having an awesome time, I was overwhelmed with the feeling that we had created this. I don't regret spending time on the details, because they all came together to make us feel loved, special, included, excited, and all manner of other cool things."

The wedding industry tells you that the details matter because they will make your wedding stand out. But that's not really true. Your place cards won't make your wedding yours; your love will. That's not to say that the details won't matter. They will, but not in the way you expect. When I think about our wedding, I remember the chocolate cake I covered in dahlias during the reception and the way my new husband and I melted into each other during a Nina Simone song (not the first dance song we'd so carefully picked). The kind of details that will stay with you are also often the things that you can never truly plan. Focus your energy on the details that get you excited. Think of those things as markers on the trail, pointing you toward your wedding joy.

ℓℓℓℓ

What You Need to Know About Wedding DIY

Let's be honest. For most of us, wedding DIY is hard work, undertaken by necessity. It involves lifting boxes, poring over spreadsheets, painstakingly crafting playlists, stripping thorns off roses, or hours and hours of cooking. Most of us don't undertake major DIY projects for our wedding because we love crafting. It's because we have a big party to throw, and this is how we can actually make it happen. So, if you're feeling overwhelmed by DIY, that is a perfectly reasonable reaction. Remember to ask for help (and lots of it). Figure out what your capacity is and try not to exceed it. Decide when you can let projects go or hire someone to help you out with them. And then ask for more help.

Over the past decade, Do-It-Yourself has snuck to the forefront of the wedding landscape. Suddenly it seems that everyone is making it from scratch, whether "it" consists of hand-painted wedding invitations or the hand-crocheted dress burning down the Internet. Handmade is suddenly such big business that there is a whole industry dedicated to helping you spend money to make "it" your own. More than that, the wedding industry has moved toward aggressive personalization, where every wedding, big or small, needs to be full of unique—and often handcrafted—details. Because no generic wedding can possibly express the depth of your love, right? (Spoiler: wrong.)

Liz Moorhead put it this way: "Our wedding was crafty and DIY, not because we're cool indie kids. Because we're broke." Modern wedding media often makes DIY sound like a trend, but for many of us it's just the reality of having a wedding. Even so, if approached rationally, DIY can lead to meaningful experiences that you might not have had with a more expensive wedding. As Liz said, "Some of, maybe all of, my favorite parts of the wedding were the result of cut[ting] corners to fit the budget." The time you spend with loved ones making your wedding happen matters and gets you ready for the day itself.

When DIYing to keep on budget, be selective about what projects you take on. No matter what you think going in, DIY does not always save you money. If you're undertaking a complicated craft that you know very little about, you might end up spending more money on supplies as you flounder around learning what you're doing than you would just hiring someone to do it for you. Before you start a project, ask yourself the following questions:

※ Is this item a must-have at our wedding?
※ Can we afford to hire someone to help us out with it?
※ If not, is it simple enough for us to take on and still stay within our budget?

(continues)

And remember, at the end of the day, you should DIY things you care about (because you will spend so many hours staring at them that they will appear in your dreams). The things you don't care about? Cut. Or if you can't cut, spend some money on it to make the problem go away forever.

In the end, your wedding is not just one day; it's the accumulation of all the moments that went into creating it. Enjoy the time you spend making your wedding happen with people you love. Try to savor the time spent cooking, or playing with flowers, or figuring out how to sew a wedding dress. Weddings are a labor of love, and when we allow the people around us to share that, sometimes we're lucky enough to create something magical (sweaty, tired, and a little bit stressed, but magical).

♧♧♧♧

> "We kept saying we didn't want a DIY wedding, because it seemed like so much work, but ultimately that's what we did, *and* we went over budget. We overestimated what we needed instead of getting professional advice, and we spent too much on cheap decor items because we had months to buy things on sale.
>
> —Angela Meriquez Vázquez, who wore a black veil at her downtown LA wedding

What Matters Most: Key Wedding Elements

Some elements of your wedding are more impactful than others. Even if you are in love with your bridesmaid dresses, your venue is going to affect the way people experience your wedding a whole lot more. Often, these high-impact facets of wedding planning don't get a lot of airplay in wedding media because they don't photograph well, or aren't expensive, or are not easy to talk about in print. But if you want to throw a lazy and chic wedding, these are the things you should focus on:

≷ **Location:** About 33 percent of your pictures will be dominated by your location. (Please note the precision with which I made this calculation.) No matter how hard you try, it's impossible to make a wedding inside a hotel ballroom look like it took place in an English garden on a warm summer day. You will save yourself a whole lot of heartache if you stop trying to force the issue and just pick a location that you like (or decide you don't care and pick one that makes the whole thing easier to plan).

≷ **The People:** For those of you following my math at home, the happy faces of the people you love will dominate the other 67 percent of your pictures. Which is to say, when you leave a great party, you're normally raving about the good time you had, not about how the favors perfectly matched the tablecloths. So, if you focus on inviting people you love, chances are good you're going to have a pretty awesome party.

≷ **The Officiant:** Have you ever been to a wedding where the officiant makes awful jokes, appears to have never met the couple in question, and robotically conducts a service that should be emotional? Yeah. You're going to want to avoid that. We'll talk more about finding the right officiant in Chapter 7, but until then, mark this choice down as "reasonably important."

≷ **The Food:** The type of food you serve sets the tone for the kind of party you want to have (and expensive food does not necessarily mean a better vibe). A sit-down steak dinner signals one thing to guests, a jazz brunch buffet reception signals something else, and rolling up with boxes of pizza with the music on blast says something else entirely. Think about your food choices and make sure they line up with the kind of party you want to throw.

≷ **The Dress/Your Killer Outfits:** We focus way too much on having the *perfect* wedding dress (because perfect isn't a real thing, even in weddings). But one of the most obvious signals you can give your guests about the type of party you're throwing is the outfit you're wearing. A slinky 1920s-style shift gives off a totally different vibe than a huge, frothy, strapless ball gown or a super-hip jumpsuit. You don't need to spend a fortune on your outfit, but you might want to fight to wear an outfit you like a lot.

≳ **The Photography:** Here is a dirty little secret: a good photographer (and I don't necessarily mean an expensive photographer) can make any wedding look stylish; a bad photographer can make the world's most expensive and chic wedding look like a hot mess. If you want to remember your wedding day as tremendously hip? Hire your photographer carefully and stop stressing about the little details.

≳ **Everything Else:** Once you've focused on getting a few key elements right, you're close to home free. Beyond that, focus only on what seems fun to you. Maybe you are looking forward to choosing the flowers. Maybe you don't care about how the wedding looks, but you want a throw-down dance party. Figure out what those elements are and do them well. If you have beautiful flowers, but no other decorations, people will remember how tasteful your wedding was. If you attempt twenty-seven craft projects, but all of them are a little bit of a mess, well, that's how it's going to look (and you are going to be a total stress ball).

ᘓᘓ

How Not to Psych Yourself Out Over Your Wedding Outfit

By Maddie Eisenhart

If wedding dress shopping were easy, there wouldn't be entire TV shows dedicated to the drama of it all. When you add the four-figure price tag and all the opinions about what you should wear to your wedding, the average human would be hard-pressed not to psych themselves out in anticipation of a trip to the wedding dress salon (and that goes double if you plan on wearing something that's not a dress to your wedding). Plus, you've most likely never shopped for something as formal as your wedding, and it probably seems like the whole world is trying to force you to cosplay as a giant cupcake. That combination of nerves and pressure can often mean walking out of the store with something that doesn't feel remotely like you. But there are a few things you can do to avoid that:

- *Don't plan on buying anything the first day you shop.* If you plan on buying a wedding outfit in a more traditional setting (a.k.a. a bridal salon) and family or friends have set aside time to join you dress shopping, there can be a lot of pressure to find "the one" and walk out with a gown that day. So if you're worried that might drive you to make choices you'll later regret, give yourself permission to do a preshopping research trip where you figure out what you like. Just tell the salespeople that you're not planning on buying anything yet and that you want to sit with your options before you commit to anything. It'll take the pressure off both of you.
- *Respect yourself.* The wedding outfit shopping experience can be heavily shaped by the individual sales associates you end up with and their personal beliefs about human bodies and wedding dresses. If you find yourself talking with someone who doesn't respect your wishes or who talks about your body in a way that makes you feel uncomfortable, it is your prerogative to ask for a new salesperson. Or to leave and choose another store altogether.
- *Say no to the dress.* Respecting yourself also means knowing if a wedding dress isn't right for you. Maybe you don't identify with traditionally feminine attire and would prefer a nicely tailored suit with a stylish bowtie and some dapper brogues. Or maybe you do want something feminine, but your version of feminine is less ball gown and more fitted jumpsuit and sequined heels. Nowhere in the Manual of Weddings does it say you have to wear a dress, let alone a big froofy white one. If your style runs more masculine of

(continues)

center, you'll be best served by a retailer who caters specifically to the Queer community (and a quick search for Queer women's suits will get you what you need there). You can just as easily pick up a men's suit, though take note: they are not typically designed for women's bodies, which can mean expensive and possibly poorly executed alterations. And if what you're after is more fashion-forward wedding attire (suit, dress, or in between), the wide world of online shopping is your oyster. Fast fashion sites tend to have affordable and modern cuts of women's suits and trend-forward outfits like sparkly jumpsuits.

❧ *Go outside your comfort zone.* Assuming you are shopping for a capital-*W* Wedding Dress, chances are you'll be dealing with several unknown quantities (What silhouettes are flattering? What fabrics do you like? What's comfortable?). Wedding dress ads in particular are notoriously bad at giving you an idea of what a dress might look like in real life. Give yourself permission to try things that feel wildly outside of your comfort zone. What you think will look good on you and what actually looks good on you can surprise you.

❧ *Styling is everything.* Wedding dresses and suits don't magically turn people into uncomfortable cake-topper versions of themselves. But a traditional gown, plus a traditional updo, plus a traditional veil (or the generic suit, plus a generic bow tie, and a generic pocket square) might make you feel like you can't recognize yourself in the mirror. If you're trying to figure out how to take a wedding outfit and make it your own, know that styling makes a huge difference. That might mean wearing your hair down with minimal jewelry and low-key makeup. Or if you want a look that's both avant-garde and traditional, wear a statement accessory that can be removed for the parts of your wedding where you want to look a little more classic and put back on when you want to party. (Wedding cape, anyone?)

Sometimes the hardest part of picking your wedding outfit is just getting out of your own head about it. But the good news is, there are so many more options for affordable, stylish, and unique wedding dresses these days (or not dresses—get down with your pantsuit, friend!) that there's no reason for anyone to end up with buyer's remorse. And P.S.—have fun.

ℓℓℓℓ

"I saw myself in a green velvet wedding dress, but that seemed weird and too out there. I'm so glad my partner was a champion of me being me, so I got to have my dream wedding outfit. (And now I'm getting it hemmed and get to wear it for pretty much every fancy occasion for the rest of my life!) I got so much pushback against this because so many people felt—and said loudly—that I would not look or feel bridal, and that I was missing out on the experience of wedding dress shopping. But I felt so beautiful and so much more like myself than I ever would have in a white gown.

—Max Devore Williams, who had an elfishly beautiful wedding in her hometown of Mendocino, California

Planning a Wedding in the Age of Social Media

It's easy to say, "I will not remember what our wedding looked like; I will remember what it felt like" (which is true). But it's hard to believe it in this age of relentless social media. Planning a wedding can feel like being constantly bombarded with pictures—in tiny little squares—of weddings that look perfect. And it's easy to get sucked in, wondering if your wedding photos will be published by your favorite wedding publication, or reposted by an amazing Instagram account that you love. It can screw with your head and make you forget that your wedding is the day you get married, and it has nothing to do with the amount of likes and comments your photos get after the fact.

So, reality check. Remember that while most photos you see on Pinterest or Instagram are meant to look effortless, they're often created by a team of professionals and then edited and curated by social media experts to look just so. But you're getting married and throwing a party, not having a photoshoot or creating a flawless Instagram feed.

Think about what matters to you and what doesn't. Unfollow social media accounts that are making you feel bad. And remember: The reason your wedding photos matter is not because there might (or might not) be one day where they get posted on the Internet. Your wedding photos matter for that day decades from now when you or someone you love takes your wedding album (or handful of wedding photos) off the shelf and looks at them and thinks, "Well, damn, these two people were so happy."

And if you decide you really do want some cute photos for the Internet (no shame in that game), here are the cheater tips:

- ⇗ Create a wedding hashtag and put it everywhere (signs, napkins, programs, you name it) so your guests will see it and use it.
- ⇗ If you're going to put effort into crafting, go big. Put your energy into creating things like big backdrops that will show up over and over again in photos. (Bonus points if you create something you can reuse throughout the day, like a ceremony backdrop that can be repurposed as a photo-booth backdrop.)
- ⇗ Pick a location (and particularly a ceremony location) that's beautiful so your photos will look good without any work on your end. That might be city hall, a pretty restaurant, or that all-pink hotel . . . but it's perfectly acceptable to decide that you want cute photos with minimal labor and pick your venue accordingly.

Mostly, try to take a mental step back and remember that pretty isn't an emotion. Focus on having a fun wedding, and the photos will sort themselves out.

Unplugged Ceremonies: Why and How

A few years ago, I got this question: A reader's uncle had videotaped her vows on his iPhone, and the day after the wedding had uploaded the video to his Facebook page and tagged her in the post. His message was that her vows were so lovely that he felt compelled to share them. She felt like her privacy had been violated. She wondered if it would be tremendously rude to ask him to take the video down. "Of course it's not rude," I replied. "What was rude was to record one of the most personal moments of someone's life and to share it as if it belonged to you."

Now, that exchange feels positively dated. These days we all take videos, photos, and more, and upload them instantaneously to social media without a second thought. We've forgotten that the person who records the event is not the person the event belongs to.

We've also all forgotten how to stay in the moment, because we're so busy documenting everything.

For one or both of these reasons, you might decide that you want an unplugged ceremony. You might not want the emotional nature of your vows shared far and wide. Or you might just want people to be emotionally present for this huge moment in your life. You might want to look out on a sea of faces you love, not the backs of iPhones. (And, heck, you might selfishly want your photographer to be able to get great photos without your mom's uncle jumping in front of them at the key moment to get a photo on his giant iPad.)

If you decide you want to get married without devices everywhere, the best plan of action is to overcommunicate this with your guests. Put it on your wedding website. Put it on a sign people will see when they walk into the ceremony. Ask your officiant to make it clear at the beginning of the service. (If you decide that you want your entire wedding unplugged, that's fine too, but you'll need to do a lot more messaging and convincing to get folks to participate—everyone wants a selfie of themselves in their wedding finest.)

And with all things wedding, prepare for imperfection. Someone is going to take a photo or a video that you don't want. Someone is going to take out their phone at the worst possible moment and jump up and take a photo. Life and weddings work like that. But don't let that stand in the way of asking for what you want and need . . . and enjoying a sacred moment . . . with (almost) no screens in sight.

Ditch the Rest

Once you've figured out which stylish wedding elements you care about, let everything else go. Repeat after me: I do not need all the things that people tell me I need. I will have a cake if I want a cake; I will have favors if I want favors; I will have flowers if I want flowers. If I do not care about these things, I will not have them, and I will not feel guilty. In fact, most of my guests will not even notice.

Trust Yourself

And finally, trust yourself. This might be the hardest wedding planning advice to follow, but it's probably the most important. When you're planning your wedding, you'll have a lot of outside input clamoring for your attention. It's easy to start thinking that there is some sort of wedding standard you need to live up to, or a particular aesthetic that's best for your wedding. This isn't true.

What's important is that you pick elements for your wedding that you like. If you're debating if this thing goes with that other thing, just remember: if you like all the items you picked for your wedding, then they've got one thing in common—they'll make you grin on your wedding day. Pick stuff that makes you happy, and then stop obsessing. Seriously. Stop it.

Use the time you gain *not* obsessing to do something worthwhile—practice for married life. Kristiina Hackel, who married for the second time in a historic home in Southern California, put it this way: "I know that a marriage, like every relationship, needs to be protected, invested in, and prioritized. You probably know this too, but let me add that the wedding is a good place to practice this. After all, you are not marrying your florist (although it may feel that way at times). Yes, the photo booth needs attention—but maybe you should just go out and see a movie instead." Got that? Now take a deep breath, step away, and go hang out with your partner. After all, this person is the reason you're in this delightful pickle in the first place.

WEDDING HOMEWORK

- Think about everyday parties that you've thrown and write a list of what you and your partner are good at, what you're not good at, and what you simply don't care about when throwing parties on the day-to-day.
- Look at your list of party-planning weaknesses and decide how to accommodate them in your wedding planning. Where will you need to ask for help? When will you need to hire help? What expectations or aspects of wedding planning do you want to get rid of entirely?
- Sit down with your partner and think about what you both have in mind when it comes to a wedding party. Try to get rid of all of the ideas about "how it should be" and figure out what you really want and need.
- Mantra for when social media starts taking over your brain: "Pretty isn't an emotion."

{6}

The Hard Stuff

ℓℓ— Beyond the Spreadsheets —ꝰ

⚶ The hardest part of wedding planning is often the conflict between what we hoped would be and what is.

⚶ A major component of the engagement process is learning to set boundaries between your family of origin and your brand-new baby family. If you find yourself fighting with family, think of it as bringing you a little closer to a new form of family harmony.

⚶ Planning a major event with your partner is going to help you develop skills for working together that you'll use for years. In the meantime, however, things might feel a little hard.

⚶ Getting married is stressful, crazy, and exciting. You're allowed to experience all these emotions and call the shots in your own wedding planning without anyone calling you a "bridezilla."

⚶ Committing to someone for the rest of your life can be terrifying. If you find yourself struggling with cold feet, try to figure out if you're scared by the idea of "forever," or if you're not sure you want to marry your partner. If it's

(continues)

129

the latter, slow everything down. Calling off a wedding is a heck of a lot easier than calling off a marriage.

≯ Your wedding is not an imposition. Grown-ups can make their own decisions about attending your wedding and how they celebrate with you. Kids will enjoy the cake and punch, regardless.

≯ If you're dealing with difficult emotions when planning, tell people exactly what kind of help you need and let them emotionally support you.

≯ Weddings represent hope, love, and the resilience of the human spirit. If there is any time that we need this kind of celebration, it's in the face of the really (really) hard stuff.

On Loss

When I first wrote this book, my husband's and my parents were all alive. In the years since, we've lost both of our fathers, my grandmother, and several other wedding guests. Looking back, all that loss makes the wedding more important. It was a moment when so many people shared our joy, including those we can't celebrate with anymore. This chapter is for those of you whose wedding planning lives outside the neat and hopeful narratives written for us by society. It's for those of you who have lost (or are losing) a loved one. It's for the folks whose families are not supportive of them or their relationship. And it's for those of you who find yourself fighting with your partner during wedding planning or are finding the transition to being part of a new family not an easy one at all.

Fighting and Crying: It's Normal

After a lifetime of books, movies, and commercials, we've fixed in our heads the idea that wedding planning is a wonderful time when everyone in our lives comes together to bond over something deeply joyful. This can make it extra difficult when reality hits and we realize it's not exactly what we imagined.

The hardest part about wedding planning is that there is almost always a conflict between what we hoped would be and what is. It's so easy to imagine that your usually emotionally distant mother is going to suddenly warm up and you will pick out wedding dresses together, giggling and weeping. You imagine that your couldn't-care-less-about-aesthetics fiancé is suddenly going to have opinions about the decor. Maybe you dream that your generally disorganized friend group is going to step up and really pitch in. Or maybe it's much deeper, and you—and all of your family—are focused on the fact that your sister who passed away isn't going to be able to be a bridesmaid (or have a wedding of her own one day). When you're hit with a reality that's different from the dream you might have had, you can end up a weepy mess, wondering if you're broken.

You're not broken. You're normal.

Wedding planning in America has become a high-stress, high-stakes, high-expense game. Even in the best of times, it's more than likely that you're going to encounter some rough patches as you navigate the process. Now, you shouldn't go looking for hard parts. As my dad used to say, "Don't borrow trouble." It is possible that you'll make it through the planning process without weeping once, particularly if you are able to start with realistic expectations and you have a laid-back family. If that happens to you, embrace it. And for goodness' sake, don't worry that you're not doing it right because you're not stressed enough. However, if you don't make it through wedding planning scot-free? Know that weddings are often hard, and crying is okay.

When I found myself a crying mess during the wedding planning process, I felt guilty. Wasn't I attempting to be a laid-back bride? But at the points in the process where I was falling apart, I was falling apart over very real, not-just-wedding-related issues. I was stressed about the realities of merging two families, or painful conflicts with friends, or issues of faith in our new family unit. These were necessary tears, growing-pains tears. Which isn't to discount the tears shed over logistics and money. Those were valid, too.

Wedding planning isn't easy. Perhaps everyone should stop pretending that it is simply an effortless romp through pretty things. In this chapter we'll discuss the fights that come up during wedding planning (they are normal), how to think through cold feet, the myth of the bridezilla (you have good reasons to be stressed), and how weddings can be a form of hope when dealing with death or otherwise absent parents. Weddings are like most good things in life: really hard and really worth it.

> **G**et your mental health in order! I was struggling with an undiagnosed anxiety disorder, and my wife was dealing with unmedicated depression, while we were planning. If we could go back in time, I would have scheduled an appointment with my doctor right after we had gotten engaged to talk about mental health and to make sure I wasn't making things harder than they needed to be.
>
> —Colleen Kimseylove, who had kittens
> at their Seattle wedding reception

Fighting with Your Loved Ones

Chances are that you're going to have some difficult moments with your family at some point during the wedding planning process. Even for those of us with generally spectacular families, things go south now and then during this high-stakes, high-emotion time period. As we've discussed, part of the point of the engagement process is learning to set boundaries between your family of origin and your brand-new baby family. Or, in other words, engagement is about fighting it out. Every fight you have over a major issue (like faith) or a seemingly minor issue (like your partner's right to overrule your mom's centerpiece choice) is one step closer to family harmony. You have two long-established families and one emerging family, and you need to figure each other out.

If you're locked in conflict with family members, it can help to look at things through their eyes. Ask questions until you figure out what the heck is going on and what they are really upset about. Brianne Sanchez, a journalist who got married on a farm west of Chicago, said, "Here's what it took me a long time to realize: I considered planning our wedding the first endeavor of Joe and mine as a new family. My mom considered the wedding the last thing a mother and a daughter do together." Ten years after my wedding, now a mother of two, I can say that the sense of loss parents are experiencing during wedding planning is very real. (How marriage will change your relationship with your family is unknown. But the emotions that many parents go through are intense, and often the mirror image of your own emotions.) Navigating this can be the hardest part of wedding planning. You may be outwardly fighting about the dress code for the wedding, but deep down you might be fighting about what level of formality is appropriate for major life events in your new family, or how hard it is for your parents that you're starting a family of your own. Even if getting married feels like a formality for you, for your parents it might feel a little bit like finally letting go of their baby (even if you're forty).

Sometimes conflict can be eased by giving parents control over an aspect of the wedding they care about (because who doesn't love a little control?). You can even let your parents do something that you would never have chosen on your own, because it matters to them. Cara Winter told me, "Let's face it—your mom has probably been looking forward to this day longer than you have. So if she begs to have welcome bags with an apple theme or to give a guided tour of Brooklyn—including places she's never actually been—realize that it's sort of her day, too.

And as long as it doesn't betray your values or steal your sanity, it's okay to let others have some control."

Your wedding, like your upcoming family life, is going to be a sometimes-tricky balance. Your job is to draw firm boundaries for things that really matter to your new family and to allow people who love you to participate by doing things they find meaningful. Don't be afraid to fight and cry, and don't be afraid of saying no when you really need to. Think of it as practice for the rest of your lives together.

Tension with Your Partner

So, you and your partner are planning a wedding together, huh? More specifically, you're planning a really large event, with complicated logistics, a big guest list, and issues of faith, values, and money right on the surface. And, for the sake of argument, let's just say you've never planned an enormous project together. But it should be easy, right? You should bond and feel deep joy, and the planning process should bring you closer together than you've ever been. Right? *Right?*

Okay. Reality check. Planning a wedding with your partner is great, in that it's going to teach you how to take on a big endeavor together. I can guarantee that you'll need these skills later in life doing things like caring for a sick parent, having kids, renovating a house, or moving across the country. But right now, things might be a little dicey. That's as it should be. As complex as it feels, planning a wedding is a relatively low-stakes way to learn how to collaborate on a stressful life project. Practice disagreeing over the guest list so you gain skills to disagree over a family member's critical care later.

The thing is, our partners often think about wedding planning a little differently than we do. My husband certainly did. It's not that he didn't care about the wedding; it was just less emotionally loaded for him. During our planning, I learned that my husband didn't have an opinion on everything, as much as I wanted him to. Sometimes he didn't want to discuss all the possible alternatives; he just wanted to think through options quickly and come to a gut-check decision. Frankly, this is something I wish I'd done more of.

If you have a partner who approaches wedding planning differently than you do, embrace it. Start figuring out the differences in how you address problems. You probably picked each other because you make each other better people. Your strategies for planning a wedding just might complement each other as well. At least, after a few fights.

The Bridezilla Myth: Making You Crazy, Then Calling You Crazy

Wedding planning has moved from being something that your family or your community does for you to being an enormous project taken on almost totally in isolation. Add that to the fact that, as discussed in Chapter 4, weddings have gotten three to four times as complicated and hugely more expensive in the course of just a few generations, and you have the recipe for disaster.

Unfortunately, none of this is being discussed in polite company—at least not in a way that women can win, at all, ever. I had conversations during wedding planning where I would be chided for being a spendthrift in the very same breath as I was chided for planning a wedding that was too casual. In addition, the people chatting with me didn't know me from Adam but felt comfortable with offering me opinions. Brides-to-be (like mothers-to-be) are perceived as a special kind of public property, which can be stressful to realize when some stranger is prattling off nonsense advice. Some people deal with this by shutting down problem conversations before they start, others try to reason with people, but some might snap and get angry. "Bridezilla" angry.

Which brings me to the madness of the term *bridezilla*. You're getting married. You're allowed to care about that. It's okay to be excited. You should feel empowered to decisively make choices that are right for you. Yes, you do have to treat people with respect and are not allowed to mindlessly boss people around (see the etiquette discussion in Chapter 4), but I suspect you're not doing that in the first place. So realize that, as a woman planning a large event, you might get accused of being controlling. You might get called a bridezilla. And that is not your issue. That's the issue of the person who feels at liberty to call you something really offensive.

Sometimes wedding planning can feel lose-lose. You're put in a very high-stress situation where the rules seem rigged, and then, when you get stressed, you're perceived as a bad person. But you're not a bad person. You're one human trying to throw an event that keeps everyone happy, while going through a major life transition. You're allowed to have opinions and make decisions. You're even allowed to get angry now and then. Why? You're the one getting married, and that gives you a few rights, along with all the responsibilities.

Cold Feet

What happens when you realize that you're planning a wedding, but you're unsure about actually getting married? Committing to a lifetime with one person is a huge thing. Sometimes the hugeness of it gets lost under the piles of to-do lists, bridesmaid dresses, and drafts of the wedding budget. Sometimes it gets lost under the modern idea that when you already live together, nothing much is going to change after getting married. Sometimes it's a panic that pulls us back to reality—getting married is a huge commitment, and not one to be taken lightly.

Forever Is . . . Terrifying

If you're freaking out about getting married, it's important to take a moment to untangle the issues (perhaps in premarital counseling, either alone or with your partner). It's important to differentiate between "I'm not sure I want to marry this person" and "Hoo-boy. Marriage is scary." If some part of you is scared of the forever nature of marriage and the possibility of divorce, this is natural. Before you walk down the aisle, it's important to acknowledge that divorce happens, and may have happened in your family.

It's easy for divorce to become the scary boogeyman in the corner, and for your fear of it to grow, as you avoid facing and talking about it. But divorce is a realistic possible outcome in marriage, and it needs to be discussed. Kimberly Eclipse was immobilized with anxiety leading up to her wedding and said, "For me, so much of being engaged was just about being brave. It was about being fully aware of the realities of marriage and signing up anyway, knowing that when the time comes, I'll fight for my relationship." If you're scared about divorce, consider it a healthy reaction. Talk about it. Talk to your partner; talk to your parents; talk to any religious figures you might have in your life. Talk to your friends. And stop thinking there is something wrong with you because you're scared.

Forever Is . . . Now

It's also possible that you're not worried about divorce but are instead panicking as you try to wrap your head around the idea of forever. And of course we freak out when we ponder questions like "How long is forever?" and "What if we don't get along in thirty years?" Those questions scare us because they don't have an answer, no matter how long we think about them, and there is nothing we can do to solve the problems they pose. They are, in a sense, totally useless (but terrifying) questions.

For some reason, I never grappled with cold feet before our wedding day. But fast-forward to our one-year anniversary, and I was freaked out. In the months leading up to our anniversary, I'd ended up in several conversations where people gave me a litany of the terrors of marriage. I spent the day of our anniversary working myself up into a near panic. What *did* forever mean? And why did it feel so claustrophobic?

Sometime during that afternoon, as the freaking out reached its peak, I had a realization: my marriage isn't for forever; my marriage is for today. All we can do is look around our life together and figure out how our relationship is doing right now. If it's good, it's good. If it's not, we can take actions to fix it. But there is nothing that can be done about thirty years from now other than to take care of each other in this moment.

It's perfectly reasonable to be a little scared about the enormity of commitment, and there are ways to deal with this trepidation. Approach the wedding one moment at a time, try to stay grounded, and focus on why you love your partner enough to make this huge commitment. And for goodness' sake, if you realize you don't want to spend the rest of your life with your affianced, be brave and call it off. No matter what books and movies tell us, getting married does not equal happiness. Getting married *to the right person* gives you a serious shot at happiness.

eeee

Everything You Need to Know About Calling Off Your Wedding

By Eve Sturges

Our wedding was going to be in my hometown at a private winery surrounded by blooming lavender fields in Northern California. Our colors were pearl and magenta, and my dress was a strapless A-line. Catering was set to cook for 150 people, the florist was secured and ready with a million magenta gerbera daisies, our Episcopalian officiant was booked, and we were working on choosing a first dance song. My mother had her dress, and his mother had booked a local Italian restaurant for the rehearsal dinner. (All of this was done, by the way, from New York before Pinterest, before text messaging, and when The Knot was brand-new and making waves with its wedding calculator.) My best friend was working on her speech. The invitations were ready to go out the following Saturday, in a box near the couch.

And then my fiancé told me he didn't want to have any more children, ever.

We canceled the wedding.

It wasn't really about whether we'd have more children. There were huge waving, screaming red flags from the beginning, and they all make this a good, juicy, exciting story. (Buy me a margarita sometime and I'll spill the beans.) But weddings are canceled for all sorts of reasons, none of which should need to be measured or justified, so I'm skipping the details. The important factor is the wave of relief that washed over me when I thought about canceling my nuptials. Relief is different from excitement; I didn't wipe my hands off and immediately move on to a Better Life. There were a lot of emotions to sift through, a lot of difficult conversations, a lot of heartbreaking questions and answers. But I focused on the relief and put one foot in front of the other.

Whether it is neon warning signs or a small achy feeling in your gut, choosing to cancel your wedding is often more stressful and scary than not, especially once the train really starts speeding toward the station. The bigger the wedding, and the closer you are to the date, the more emotion and money are invested from all around you. For me there was a lot of pressure to get married because we'd had a baby, and I was choosing to walk away from the action that would essentially have righted the error of my ways. Also, my partner loved me and loved our daughter; there were a lot of reasons it "made sense" to get married. But it was better to struggle as a single mom and face down my family's moral opinions than to make a legal, financial, celebratory, religious commitment to a life in which I was not happy.

People still tell me that it was a brave thing to cancel my wedding. I didn't especially feel heroic about it, but it's a concept I've mulled over for more than ten years now, and I think I underestimate the pressure placed on engaged couples to seal the deal. I am not pro or anti cancel, but I know there are people out there who are worried about the small voice inside begging them to wait, and I wish there were more readily

(continues)

available resources to help people figure out what that voice means. Based on my experience, and the frightening variables that make this feel overwhelming, these are the pieces of guidance that I wish were available to me when I was weighing the options and questioning "I do."

You Will Survive

Everyone survives these things. I'm sure that, deep down, you already know this. The discomfort—the embarrassment, the tears, the unknown—can feel excruciating, but it will pass. I felt overwhelming relief when the wedding was canceled, but it also took a long time for me to find a new normal.

Find Support, but Not from Your Partner

Ask someone who is close to you for some extremely confidential quality time. If no one comes to mind who can offer unbiased and open-minded listening skills, see if you can find a therapist in your area. Religious leaders often offer counseling, so maybe the officiant of your wedding is a good bet. Even look for an online forum; anything is better than nothing. There will be a time to talk with your fiancx, but right now you need a neutral zone.

It Isn't About Love

It is absolutely possible and acceptable to love someone and still decide that marriage is not the right path for the two of you. It's also possible to feel incredibly loved by your fiancx and also feel like marrying isn't the right direction. Marriage is about more than love. Marriage is about all aspects of life: finances, children, dreams, career, health and safety, freedom, and happiness. If you can't identify what the nagging feeling is now, I bet that you'll figure it out eventually, so don't ignore it just because it doesn't fall into a particular category.

Don't Let the Logistics Overwhelm You

This is where support is crucial. I sent a list of vendors to my parents, who called or visited each and every one in our small town. A lot of them were happy to refund the deposits, and those that didn't offer refunds allowed us to use them as credit at their businesses. Later in the year, I used the photographer for some family pictures, and we sent flowers to people who had helped during that uncomfortable transition.

Instead of those pretty invitations, we mailed out plain postcards with a simple sentence: "The wedding between Eve and Jim has been postponed indefinitely." That was the wording my mother was most comfortable with, and it got the job done. There was no need for any lengthy explanations or apologies. If we had been even closer to the wedding, we would have phoned everyone (in fact, I am sure we did phone some people to make sure they got the news). People have plane tickets and hotel reservations to cancel, and it's better they know sooner as opposed to later. If it feels too scary or hard to know what to say, write it down and read a script that keeps your uncle in North Dakota from asking too many questions.

Be sure to surround yourself with people who can help— get your bridesmaids to put that crafting energy into new tasks, whether it's to sit with you and stamp postcards, check names off the list, pour you a glass of wine, or split the guest list with you to deliver the news.

Maybe Most Important, There Are No Wrong Decisions Here

One of my favorite passages ever is in a book from the Twelve-Step community: "Shame never lifted a single spirit." It is all right to cancel a wedding. It is all right to get married and decide later on that it was a mistake; you will learn and grow from each experience. It may be that this marriage will last a lifetime and you can chalk these hesitations up to cold feet; only you will know when you know. I ignored signs until I didn't, and then I got through the fallout, sometimes gracefully, often haltingly. Remember that no matter what, it will all be okay.

ഇഇഇ

Your Wedding Is Not an Imposition

In recent years, I've watched people become increasingly worried that their wedding is an imposition and then try to do everything they can to throw a wedding without inconveniencing a single person. (Spoiler: that's not even possible.) But even still, your wedding is not an imposition.

Did you get that? It's not an imposition on *anyone*. I know, people will have to travel, or spend money, or spend time, or do something slightly outside their comfort zone, and you're not sure if you're within your rights to ask them to do that. But you are.

Your wedding is not an imposition, not because your guests will have fun at your wedding (though they will), but because your guests are grown people. Got that? They are *grown-ups*. Your wedding guests are adults and should be treated as such. They can make their own decisions as to their attendance, they can book their own travel, they can buy you gifts on their own, and they can pick their own clothes. And because they made every single one of these decisions on their own, you are not imposing on them in any way. Your wedding is a party that they are delighted to attend. If your wedding is too expensive, or too far away, or just too much of a bother? They won't come. Hopefully, they'll be kind about it when they tell you they can't come. But if not, you probably didn't want them there in the first place. Marisa-Andrea Moore Shelby, who got married in a small ceremony in her parents' backyard in Southern California, said, "The people who love you and care about you will not feel like your wedding is a burden or an imposition. They will be thrilled that out of all of the people you could have invited, you want *them*." People are coming to your wedding because they love you, and they want an excuse to celebrate this happy event in your life. Your wedding is not an imposition. Your wedding is a joy.

Planning a Wedding When Life Hurts

There are times when life is so hard that planning a wedding can feel utterly frivolous. During a painful moment in our wedding planning, I came across this quote from Elie Wiesel, which forever changed my perception of why we have weddings. In his book *A Jew Today* he says, "In our tradition, celebration of life is more important than mourning over the dead. When a wedding procession encounters a funeral procession in the street, the mourners must halt so as to allow the wedding party to proceed. Surely you know what respect we show our dead, but a wedding, symbol of life and renewal, symbol of promise too, takes precedence." In that moment, I realized what every older adult already knows. Weddings are about hope. Weddings are hope for the future, hope for a new generation, and the hope that love and family can win over everything else. Weddings are not more important than life, nor do they stand apart from life, but they represent something bigger than us, something larger than the dress we wear or the flowers we carry. So on the days it seems too hard to go on, too hard to pick flowers in the face of grief or pain, remember the why of weddings. When life leaves us a puddle on the floor, weddings allow us a reason to hope and give us a brief shining moment in the sun. They allow us to celebrate who we love with the people we love, which is always, always, necessary.

Weddings and Grief

More often than we'd like to think, weddings come face-to-face with grief. Maybe a parent has died and you're planning without them, or maybe someone you care deeply about is in the process of dying. How do we face this? How do we reconcile great joy in the face of great loss?

Each day since my husband and I lost our fathers, we've had to face what it looks like to keep living and keep celebrating milestones when someone you love isn't there to share them. So for those of you planning weddings with a family member dying, or for those of you grappling with the absence of critical family members while you walk down the aisle, I want to assure you that you are far from alone.

Over the decade plus that I've written about weddings, I have spoken to so many people who were trying to feel their way through the process of celebrating one of life's biggest milestones while dealing with grief. And while these stories rarely make it into wedding media, movies, or even commercials, many people are grappling with the same terrible issues.

> **M**y mom won't help me pick out the dress. She won't be there to help decide on flowers. She won't be there to stay up until two a.m. writing envelopes for our Save the Dates. She won't see me walk down the aisle. But she did give me her blessings so long ago when I naturally started talking about marrying Kyle. She did help me wedding plan even before we were officially getting married. And she is with me through all of these moments.
>
> —Darci Flynn, whose mom died
> before she got engaged

A Dying Parent or Loved One

If you are engaged and you have a parent or loved one who is dying, the central question is usually: Do you move up the wedding so they can be there for it, or do you keep the wedding plans as they are? I spoke to one person who did both and was able to offer insight into what each experience was like for her. She married her husband in a ceremony over her father's hospital bed. A few months after her father died, the couple held another celebration with a wedding dress and party. She told me that on her wedding day she could only think about how she was about to lose her dad, so it was one of the saddest days of her life. While she was glad that her father was able to see them married, it turned out that their second celebration was necessary because it was just that: a celebration. It allowed her to enjoy her wedding the way her dad would have wanted her to. There is, of course, no one right answer to how and when to plan your wedding with a dying loved one. You, your partner, your family, and your loved one will need to decide what option seems best, knowing that no solution will fix what is broken or take the pain away.

ՉՉՉՉ

A Wedding in the Face of Death

By Morgan Turigan

It was a hard year. In March, my partner, David, learned that he was "temporarily out of work," and my father informed me that he had stage IV lung cancer. Then they discovered cancer in Dad's brain, and he started chemo and radiation. David's return to work was delayed. In July, we decided on a whim to go to Scotland and Ireland. David proposed at a Neolithic portal tomb, and it was wonderful. We started to plan a wedding and figured that March, six months away, seemed safe. David went back to work after eight months as my father's health declined. We knew that it would be my father's last Christmas, and we tried to paste on smiles. Wedding plans progressed, but it was hard to care.

My father died fifty days before the wedding.

I have very few memories of the week between his death and the wake. I do know that the day after he died, David and I bought a house, and we were stuck with possession the weekend before the wedding. We packed up, conned friends to help us move, and ate a lot of takeout. The wedding was wonderful. We went on a lazy beach honeymoon and came home to start setting up house.

A week later, my nineteen-year-old cousin died of a totally unexpected heart problem. He was the spitting image of my father, to the point that at Dad's wake I'd made a joke that

(continues)

as long as we had Michael, it would feel a little bit like young Dad was around. So. Things were hard. The big stuff was very, very hard.

I didn't necessarily cope well. I stopped sleeping. I drank too much rum. I closed the door to my office and cried. The night before my father died, after I left the hospital in the middle of the night, I screamed the entire way home, and my voice was left hoarse and raw for a week. I leaned on David—hard—and he caught me when I crumpled. I had anxiety attacks. I made spreadsheets to quell the wedding anxiety. In some ways, having the wedding to focus on was a small blessing—it was a series of tasks that needed to be done. Unlike watching my father die in slow motion, where there was nothing to do but watch and grieve.

I got grief in waves, and I was fine on the wedding day. The next day? Tired and exhausted and hungover? I made it through the wedding brunch, made it partway home, and then I started to cry. I cried for the next two hours, finally crying myself to sleep in David's arms. My grief came, in part, from managing to get through the wedding without my father, and in part because rites of passage really are a big deal, no matter how happy they make you.

People advised me to move up the wedding date, or to involve my father in the planning. That just didn't work for us. Up to the week before he died, my mother was sure that he would make it, and I got the feeling that he knew he wouldn't. He lived long enough to meet my husband and to see me happy, and for that I am ever so blessed.

We made sure to celebrate his memory in small ways on the day, and it helped. I wore my father's blue star sapphire engagement ring. The pastor talked about loss and families. My sister's original toast was about my dad, but she wasn't able to handle it, and told a funny story about me instead. David's toast to my father made people tear up.

Do I wish my dad was there? Of course. Do I wish he had lived and suffered through a horrible and humiliating illness for two more months just to have watched me wed? Of course not. Do I have any regrets about throwing the wedding, about the timing, about our choices? Sure, everyone has regrets, but I can live with my choices. Do I regret standing up in a room full of family and friends and declaring my love? No, absolutely not. Life is short, and it can be cruel; we all know this, so any excuse to celebrate joy should be taken.

Managing to sandwich the wedding in between two funerals makes it abundantly clear to me just how important weddings are. I felt tremendously loved by my family at the wake and the wedding, but the joy at the wedding was healing and wonderful. Talking about grief and death is hard. Celebrating joy in the face of grief is hard, and ever so necessary.

ഉരൂൂ

Planning Without a Parent

Part of the enduring myth of wedding planning is that it is one of life's great mother-daughter bonding rituals. And even in good parent-child relationships, wedding planning can be more complicated than books and movies might lead you to believe. But this process can be infinitely more difficult if you have a parent who is absent from your life. The challenges are different depending on the situation—your parent may simply not be part of your life, may be choosing to not be part of your wedding, or may be emotionally unavailable to you. And of course, it's a whole other complicated puzzle if you've lost a parent. Each of these situations can be terrifically hard, and in their own way each one can leave you grieving for what you deserve—the love, presence, and support of your parent.

An Emotionally Absent Parent

One bride, who had a mother who was unable to support her through the process and a father who had died, told me, "Having an emotionally absent parent is hard. In some ways, it can be harder than having a dead parent, because then you can keep hoping for a change, and there's always a chance for a new hurt. Having one of each? I wish neither on anyone." She offered important advice: let yourself grieve. It can be hard to feel like you're allowed to grieve the loss of an experience with a parent who is still alive. But if you have a parent who is ill, or emotionally unable to reach out to you, accept that as a loss of what you'd hoped for and let yourself feel that pain. And then work to take care of yourself and protect your heart. Maybe this means having a bridesmaid run interference with your parent, or maybe it means working with your partner to reset your expectations to something more realistic. But don't beat yourself up for your feelings, whatever they are. You're grieving a very real loss.

Planning After the Death of a Loved One

For those of you planning a wedding after the loss of a parent or loved one, I am so sorry. There is, of course, nothing that will make that loss better, but knowing that other people are going through it as well can make you feel less alone. Lynn Schell wrote that planning her wedding a few years after her mother died was "a sickening cycle of excitement and joy followed—approximately eight hours later—by overwhelming grief and anger." She said, "I just couldn't handle the emotional roller coaster of loving the feeling of getting married, only to be followed by the sheer devastating disappointment that Mom wouldn't be there to play silly games and make a teary-eyed toast. It was like losing her all over again; only again, and again, and again, and again." As all of you who have lost someone know, there are no magical solutions to grief. And as it teaches us time and time again, there is no way out but through. Nothing is going to bring your loved one back.

Lynn told me that what saved her, in the end, was learning that her partner was not going to understand her feelings unless she told him. She said, "When I finally gave up hoping he would get it, and finally started saying simply 'I miss my mom' every time I felt it, we got on the same page about how complex and difficult a daughter-sans-mother existence can be." You miss your loved one. That's not ever going to go away. Allow yourself to tell people what you need, even if it's nothing other than a shoulder to cry on, and let them support you. As for your partner, at best this can be a chance for them to learn how to support you, because this loss will always be part of you and your story.

Sometimes You Can't Get What You Need (but If You Try, You Can Get What You Want)

If a loved one isn't around to emotionally support you through wedding planning, it's important to realize early on that you can't expect someone else to completely fill in for them. As Lynn told me, "Your bridesmaids are not your mother. Your partner is not your mother. Your father is not your mother." But when in crisis, get help, even if that means hiring someone. She explains that you need to find "candidates who can be 'mother-by-proxy,' who you can sit down with and really explain what you need during this time. For me it was unconditional positive affirmations, constant and boundless energy, and the desire to make this the best party ever." Once you realize that no one can step into the void of the missing loved one, you can start identifying specific areas where you need help. The bride with the emotionally absent mother told me, "No one can replace your mother—for better or worse, she's your mom. But! People can replace her in tasks that traditionally fall to the mother-of-the-bride. I am lucky, and I have an amazing mother-in-law, who did things like organizing breakfast on the wedding day and talking me off (planning-related) ledges and telling me I looked beautiful." People want to support you, because they know you are dealing with a loss, and because it's your wedding day, damn it. But you need to tell them that you need help, and then tell them exactly what you need. Maybe you need someone to go wedding dress shopping with you, but you know that you're going to sob it out afterward because your mom wasn't there. You know you need someone to pat you on the back for twenty minutes while you cry and then take you out to lunch and make you laugh. Tell them that. People can't guess what your needs are before you figure them out yourself, but you're allowed to tell them how to help. I swear to it.

The Power of Weddings

Over the years, the number-one piece of advice people dealing with serious pain while wedding planning have given me is this: have a wedding. The power of bringing people together in joy, particularly in a time of sorrow, is power that cannot be underestimated. Caitlin Driscoll Cannon, whose mother-in-law died rather suddenly of cancer the same week as their wedding, said, "I thought we should cancel, but as soon as I uttered the words a wave of no's from both sides of the family drowned out my hesitations. And so, we had a wedding. And that's what mattered. That in the midst of the saddest week of our lives, we were joining our families and friends to say: this is hard, but there is still joy. And we've learned that a wedding is not just 'your day'; it is a day to celebrate the lives you were born into, the ones you've made, the ones you continue to build."

There is no right timing for a wedding when you're grieving. You may be ready to do it right away—or you may need to wait till you have some time to breathe or start the slow process of wading through your pain. But when the time is right, try to hold space for the fact that a celebration of life is important, particularly when we are bearing witness to the endless loss that is death.

Weddings are bigger and more powerful than we understand when we're planning them. They represent hope, love, family, and the resilience of the human spirit. That may sound like something off a Hallmark greeting card, but it's true. Weddings are a moment when we can celebrate life in all of its transience and imperfection, and if there is any time when we need that celebration, it's in the face of the really (really) hard stuff.

WEDDING HOMEWORK

- If the reality of wedding planning isn't feeling how you hoped it would, give yourself space to process that. Write down how you'd hoped things would be. Then write about how things actually are right now. Allow yourself to feel whatever emotions come up.

- Is wedding planning getting stressful? Totally normal, and you don't have to go through this alone. Consider finding a therapist, if you don't have one already. Couples counseling—premarital or otherwise—is great, and I recommend it prewedding. Sometimes you need someone who listens to you once a week and can help you advocate for yourself.

- When wedding planning is a dance with grief, or brings you face-to-face with difficult family dynamics, sit down and talk to your partner about it. If you can, come up with a list of times you know you'll need extra support, and then set up a game plan for those moments. (Also know that grief is unpredictable, and those plans might have to be thrown in the trash at some point.)

- Mantra when things get hard: "Weddings let us celebrate life in all of its transience and imperfection."

7

The Ceremony

⌇⸺ Beyond the Spreadsheets ⸺⸚

- ⸙ The ceremony is where you do the really important bit—
  get married. Give it the attention it deserves, whether
  you're writing a ceremony from scratch or making small
  adjustments to a traditional service.
- ⸙ The fundamental building blocks of your ceremony are
  your beliefs. Take time to discuss them, whether religious
  or secular, with your partner. Don't avoid disagreements.
  They can be a rich foundation for your marriage.
- ⸙ When looking for an officiant, remember that you want to
  find someone you like, on a gut level. This person will be
  ushering you into the institution of marriage.
- ⸙ If you're using a traditional service, think about why this
  service is meaningful to you, and approach it with intention
  and emotion. If you do this, your ceremony will be anything
  but boring.
- ⸙ When writing your own vows, allow time to craft something simple and meaningful. When using traditional vows,

(continues)

consider the power of using the same words spoken by the many generations who have gone before you.

⁊ Once you've crafted your ceremony, show up emotionally.

The Ceremony: Making the Vows That Change You

When planning your wedding, it's tempting to skip right over the ceremony. It seems like the part that doesn't need any attention; there are not a lot of logistics, and it's easy to find someone who will just tell you what you need to do. This is a mistake. Marchelle Farrell, who lives in the United Kingdom but held her wedding in her native Trinidad, noted, "The heart and soul of a wedding is the ceremony. It's when you do that really important bit—get married. Really think with your partner about what it means to you both to get married, and then try to let that show in your ceremony." The ceremony is the core reason everyone is gathered. You're vowing to spend your life with another person, and that's huge. Give it the attention it deserves, whether you are writing it from scratch or merely making adjustments to a traditional service.

Think of it this way: if you create a really meaningful wedding ceremony, you can put less effort into the rest of the party. If your guests are on an emotional high after basking in your love and wiping away their tears, they are much less likely to notice that the centerpieces never showed up. Writing a meaningful ceremony is the lazy person's way of avoiding too much focus on the details of the reception.

Maybe you're constructing a ceremony from scratch, or maybe you're having a traditional service. In this chapter, we'll discuss ways of making the service meaningful, selecting an officiant, and thinking about the vows you'll make. And finally, we'll dive into the big question:

How will it feel? Maybe it will feel gritty, maybe transcendent, maybe like nothing much, but probably totally surprising.

Issues of Faith

Your beliefs are a fundamental building block of your ceremony, whether they are religious or secular. Perhaps you, your partner, and your family share a cohesive set of values. If not, well, join the club. Discovering the realities of what you and your loved ones hold as truth is part of the reason that you go through the engagement process. You are starting a brand-new family, and it's important to figure out what your values are, even when that's complicated.

Secular Versus Religious

You would think that the choice between a secular and a religious wedding would be an easy one. "We go to church!" "We don't go to church!" Done.

You would be wrong.

Questions of faith in families are complicated, and weddings often bring up deep-seated issues. Your parents may not have darkened the door of a church since your baptism and suddenly insist that they are deeply religious people and your wedding will not be valid if it's not in a church. Tricky.

What do you do? First, talk to your partner. Your first responsibility is to the spiritual life of the family you are going to create. Don't start your married life on a foundation of something you think is false. If the idea of a religious wedding is anathema to either you or your partner, you need to have a conversation with your parents. You need to explain to them that the wedding is the first part of defining your new family's traditions and ethics; religion and/or God is not going to have a place in the spiritual life of your family, but you still love and respect their choices. This conversation is not going to be an easy one. But you need to have this conversation at some point, and sooner is better than later.

Second, stay flexible. Maybe you and your partner are not personally active in your parents' faith, but honoring their cultural legacy is important to you. If so, be open to that. Christen Karle Muir was initially upset at her parents' insistence that her wedding take place in a Catholic church, but in the end came to terms with it. She said, "At first it frustrated me that my parents would not budge, but I understood their position—it is their faith and my upbringing, and I am grateful for it. I am spiritual in my own way and use tools from a Catholic foundation to create my own multifaceted, nondenominational approach to the mysteries of life. Nonetheless, I am inescapably a Catholic at heart. Life, love, and the spirit are complicated, and this is who I am." For many of us, grappling with faith issues during wedding planning allows us a chance to make peace with what we believe and why. That's a gift (even if it feels painful at the time).

Interfaith Weddings

If you and your partner don't share a faith background, you have the advantage of conflict being right out in the open. While I know this doesn't always make you feel lucky, try to embrace it. There are wedding books that will tell you that having an interfaith wedding is exciting and easy because you have two whole faiths to choose from (lucky you!). But as someone who had an interfaith wedding process, I can tell you this is a bit of an idealistic take on things. Dealing with two faith systems is complicated and deserves a book of its own (see "Selected Sources," page 201, for some recommendations), but it's almost never easy.

If you haven't had a long talk about your personal values systems and how those intersect with your personal religious practices, now is the time to do that. What values do you share? Where are your beliefs different? Don't avoid the places that you disagree, as those conversations can provide a rich and complex foundation for your marriage.

Then, move on to a discussion of your religious backgrounds and how you want them to shape your family life and your wedding service. Do you want an interfaith service, or a service of just one faith? Remember, there is no right answer to this question, and thoughtful disagreement might unearth fascinating things about how your partner thinks about religion. If you decide you want an interfaith service, explore the realities of what that might look like. Will your religious leaders officiate an interfaith service? Will your families of origin be comfortable with this kind of service? The key is to strike a balance between something that works for each of you and something that makes sense in the context of your religious beliefs. If you begin a conversation about faith and religion that you'll continue for the rest of your lives, that's wedding planning time well spent.

Finding an Officiant

Once you've decided on the basic faith constructs of your wedding, it's time to find an officiant. If you're having a religious ceremony, your options may be somewhat constrained. If you're having a secular ceremony, your options may be terrifyingly wide open. But the most basic question you should ask yourselves about any officiant is simply: Do I like this person? Do I, on a gut level, like them and want them to usher me into the institution of marriage? If you don't, move on. If you do, here are some questions to help you start a dialogue with your potential officiant:

- Will you work with us to help construct a ceremony and select readings and music that make the traditional ceremony meaningful to us?
- Will you provide premarital counseling? If not, can you provide us a list of books about marriage that would be helpful for us to read and discuss?

≋ Can you tell us about wedding ceremonies you've performed that you found particularly moving?

≋ Are you comfortable with the elements we are planning on using for our ceremony? (If not, why not? Sometimes what you'll learn will change your mind.)

≋ What is your definition of marriage?

≋ Will you work with us to create vows, or to find a way to make the traditional vows meaningful to us?

≋ What do you wear when you perform a wedding?

≋ Will you help guide us through the time before our service? What thoughts do you have on helping couples enter the service in a grounded and focused way? (Translation: If I totally freak out before I walk down the aisle, are you going to pat me on the back and tell me to breathe? Because you'd better.)

≋ Do you stay after the service and socialize at the reception? Why or why not?

≋ Or, if you're asking a friend to perform your service, ask: Is this something you are comfortable doing? Why would you like to officiate for us?

Once you've met with one or two (or six) officiants and asked some of the above questions, sit down with your partner and focus on the most important question of all: Whom do you like? Whom do you trust? Whom do you want standing next to you when you say your vows? Let that guide your selection. And if you have very limited choices because of your faith, remember, it's wonderful to work with a practiced officiant within a tradition that's had meaning for thousands of years.

Constructing Your Own Ceremony

Writing a ceremony can seem exciting and liberating, while feeling terrifying and overwhelming at the exact same time. Start by building a foundation. Caitlin Helms, who was married in Duluth, Minnesota, said, "Before you write a ceremony, I think you need to figure out what you believe about marriage fundamentally." Take this opportunity to discuss what marriage means to you. Once you've figured that out, let it stand as a mission statement for your ceremony.

Here is the closely guarded secret of writing a wedding service: you don't really need to write your ceremony from scratch. In fact, it may be impossible to write it from scratch. After all, you're choosing to join an institution with a history that spans thousands of years. Chances are, you're not going to reinvent the wheel. Realize that part of what's beautiful about marriage is its universality and take some pressure off yourself to create the perfect, personalized service. You're just trying to create something that's honest.

Start by looking for a service structure that reflects your basic views about marriage. Maybe it's the Episcopal wedding liturgy, or the civil ceremony as performed in your country; maybe it's something you find further afield. Just find something that has a ring of truth for you. Once you have picked the frame you'll use to structure your service, discover your relationship to it. As you look at the ceremony, there are probably going to be bits that each of you dislike, and other parts that one or the other of you finds very important. You may be surprised by which parts of the service get an emotional reaction from one or both of you, so be careful with yourself and go slowly. Take things out that don't work. If you have a really strong emotional reaction to something, try to figure out why. This will help you shape your service (and marriage), and help you discover how close or how far you want to be from your particular version of tradition.

Once you've ironed out a basic service structure, it's time to consider adding in things that you love. If you ask me, this is the fun part. Collect a list of readings and music that you might want to use and start fitting them into your structure. From there, tweak, adjust, play, polish. Consider how long you want the service to be, or how short. Question assumptions: Does the bride have to walk down the aisle? Do either of you have to walk down the aisle? Heck, do you want an aisle in the first place? Whatever you do, remember to keep a sense of play.

Making a Traditional Ceremony Your Own

You're getting married in a house of worship, or you're having a standard civil ceremony, and you're going to celebrate your wedding with time-honored traditions. Excellent. First, let's dispel the popular myth that traditional ceremonies are boring. If a traditional service is part of who you are, then that service is going to be emotional and personal and real. There is no quicker way to make a ceremony boring than for the couple to think it's a little dull, so let go of that idea right now.

When you're working within the confines of a more traditional service, think of the age-old structure as a vessel. It's something that you're going to fill up with emotion, with your personalities, with family, and with the love that you have for each other. And the older the service, the stronger the vessel.

So, how do you fill up your wedding service? How do you take a bunch of words that you didn't pick and make them your own? Here are some ideas:

- **Intention.** Why are you having a traditional wedding in the first place? Maybe it's important to you personally. Maybe it's significant to your parents, and you've realized that honoring them is a key part of who you are. Whatever the reasons, think about them and talk them through with your partner.
- **What does it all mean?** Next, start looking at the service together. It's really easy to gloss over words you've heard a million times, but stop doing that. Look at the words of your service and talk about them. What do they mean to each of you personally? If your wedding service just seems like a bunch of boring words to you, it's going to put your guests to sleep. If your wedding service is a bunch of really meaningful and specific words, you'll make your guests cry.

≋ **Thoughtfully add music and readings.** Almost all traditional services have room for you to add and subtract readings and music. When the bulk of your service is set, it's important to really think about your choices. Religious and time-honored texts and musical traditions have so much rich and amazing material to choose from, you could spend a lifetime picking.

≋ **Value your choices.** Stop writing your wedding off as "boring" or "traditional." If you fill up the vessel of tradition with yourselves, I'm pretty sure that's as good as it can possibly get.

≋ **Show up.** If you show up, if you're fully emotionally present, if you've thought carefully about the choices you've made? Well. I'll be the person in the back bawling.

Vows: Personal and Traditional

If the ceremony is the core of the wedding, then the core of the service is your vows. This is the moment when you make promises to each other, in front of witnesses, and vow to bind your lives together forever. So, you know, no small thing. Take some time to think about the words you're going to say, whether they are traditional or nontraditional. Weigh them on your heart and let them change you. Whatever you say, make it simple, personal, and yours. Let that be the detail of the wedding that matters and be what you remember forever.

Writing Your Own Vows

Writing your own vows is an excellent opportunity to sit down with your partner, discuss what marriage means for you, and allow that to be reflected in the promises you make. First, ponder what form you want your vows to take. Do you want them to be a personal discussion of your relationship, or a more universal statement on what marriage means to you? Do you want them to be something you write in secret, or something you craft together as a thoughtful statement about your partnership? One bride I spoke to was told by her officiant that his concern with self-written vows was that they were not usually promises, and that even when they were, often people did not make equal pledges to each other. He suggested constructing vows that were one set of promises repeated by each person. Maddie Eisenhart and her husband, who married in a low-key service on a public beach in Maine, each wrote their own vows. They took the form of statements about their shared history, their hopes for the future, and the promises they were making to each other. Vows can come in any number of forms, but I would encourage you to root them in discussion and take your time writing them.

Remember that it's okay to keep things simple. The act of making enormous promises to another person is, in itself, a statement of love. Vows do not always need to be in the form of a love letter to another person; they can be short or simple pledges. And try not to pressure yourself to make jokes. There is a time and place for jokes at a wedding: during the toasts, when everyone is a little tipsy. Let your ceremony be a place for unvarnished truth, for digging deep and speaking about what is really important to you. As Maddie Eisenhart told me, "Nothing is going to make your vows as powerful as really saying, quite simply, why the hell it is you're getting married." Whatever you write, let it be a statement of your core values, of what you believe your marriage to be.

My vows referenced how I came so far from being a gay man feeling lost in his teens with *no* role models on successful gay relationships or weddings to having my dreams come true. Instead of throwing a bouquet, we threw a boa . . . naturally!

—Matthew Bollinger, who married his husband
at a wedding in the forest that looked like
it was plucked from the pages of *Vogue*

Time-Honored Vows

If you're getting married in a religious setting, chances are that you'll be required to use time-honored vows. Or maybe you can't quite get comfortable with the idea of writing your own vows. If that's the case, I'm going to toss this idea out there: don't. Getting married means joining in a tradition that is thousands of years old. By saying the same words that generations and generations before you have said, you tie yourselves to the strength of an institution that has stood the test of time, helped people survive great hardships, and helped them embrace enormous joy. Like a traditional ceremony, your vows will have emotion and meaning if you think about them, and discuss them, and know what you're saying and why. The timelessness of the words you say will only add power.

Transcendent or Not: The Gritty, Real Onceness of It

I would describe the thirty-minute process of actually getting married as transcendent, in a literal way. The definition of transcendent is "extending or lying beyond the limits of ordinary experience," or "being beyond the limits of all possible experience and knowledge." Our wedding ceremony was not the happiest moment of my life, nor was it perfect. I didn't feel like a fairy princess; I didn't even tear up much. Instead, it felt gritty and raw. It felt like something I'd never experienced before and like something I probably would never experience again. It felt outside the bounds of ordinary experience. In the end, all I can say is that I felt different walking down the aisle than I felt walking back up. For me, getting married was transcendent, but not in a glowy, magical way. Anna Shapiro said, "Transcendent moments are not about perfection or joy, or fairy tales coming to fruition; rather, they're about moments of powerful realization about the world that we are a part of and forces that are much bigger than us." And that is what a thoughtful wedding service can do. It can tie us to the greater human experience and to a larger institution. There is power in making huge commitments in front of a community of witnesses (whether two or two hundred). As Anna Alter, a bride who had a summer camp–style wedding, told me, "People said it felt like everyone got married that day. Our community lifted us up in a way that was so humbling, it really hit me after it was all over that *this* is why people have weddings." The best you can do is to think about your ceremony and prepare something that is thoughtful and feels like a reflection of who you are. After that, you just show up.

WEDDING HOMEWORK

- Sit down together and separately write down the definition of what marriage means to you. Compare what you wrote and discuss what you want *your* marriage to mean. Write down a joint definition.
- Then write down a statement of each of your beliefs around faith, spirituality, or general values. Again, do this separately, and then look at them together and see if you can come up with a joint statement of belief or values.
- Looking at those definitions, talk about how you want to reflect those ideas in your wedding ceremony.
- Talk about who you want officiating your wedding: A friend? A hired officiant? A clergy member? Think about the advantages and disadvantages of each option, and discuss what will work best for the wedding ceremony you're starting to build.
- If you don't want to write your own vows, look at the traditional vows that you're choosing to say. Discuss what they mean to you and what's important to you about them.
- If you're going to write your own vows, sit down and write a list of promises that you want to make to the other person. As with your other lists, see if you can come up with a joint list of promises that you both want to commit to. Consider using this as the basis of your wedding vows.
- Talk about (or look for) the basic ceremony structure that you're planning on using. Regardless of your starting point,

think about what you might want to add or subtract. That might be as simple as hymn and prayer choices, or as complicated as deciding you want to get matching tattoos during the service. Whatever you're adding, think about what value it has to you and how it feeds into your ideas about the marriage you are creating.

Mantra when thinking about your ceremony: "I don't know how any of this will feel, but I'm open to experiencing what is."

8

One Wonderful, Wildly Imperfect Day

ᴄᴄ —— Beyond the Spreadsheets ——ɔ ᴐ
(Okay, This One Is Kind of About Spreadsheets)

⋗ Expect imperfection. The things that go wrong are what make the day yours.

⋗ Well-laid plans allow you to have a more chill wedding day, so do your planning homework.

⋗ Remember to ask for help. You can't plan or execute a wedding alone, nor should you have to.

⋗ Come up with a system to organize your wedding planning information early in the process. Having everything organized in spreadsheets that you can pass off (or whatever high-tech solution you come up with) will let you experience the emotion of the day.

⋗ Create a detailed day-of timeline that outlines who is doing what and when on your wedding day.

⋗ Hand over all of this information to a wedding stage manager (a.k.a. a friend you owe a lifetime of free drinks) or a day-of coordinator the day before your wedding.

(continues)

> ❧ Consider appointing a few emotional bodyguards, whose job it is to keep all stress and drama away from you.
> ❧ Remember: Weddings can be stressful. If you find yourself wanting to kill someone, that's normal. Allow yourself to let it go and walk away.
> ❧ Set a no-stress deadline where you say "f*ck it," and move from the planning to the doing.
> ❧ You get to choose how to react when things go wrong. Choose to let them go, at least for one day.
> ❧ Your wedding day may not feel how you expected it to feel. Try to embrace that.
> ❧ The great thing about weddings is that you can't ruin them . . . because your wedding will lead to your marriage. And that's the whole point.

Surviving Your Wedding (Sane)

If you're reading this book, chances are very good that you've been called a bride for months and months. (Sadly, this is likely true even if you don't identify as a bride, because society hasn't figured out less gendered language for weddings yet.) But regardless of wording, the truth is you're not currently a bride, or even a person getting married. Not yet, anyway. That part only happens on your actual wedding day.

For most of us, the liminal state of getting married lasts for about ten hours. It's long enough to put on your wedding outfit, say the vows, transform yourself from a single person to part of a brand-new family, and party like it's going out of style. Then it's over, and that's a good thing. So, rather than lament the end of our short-lived moment as a person getting hitched, the question is how we take those hours and experience them to their fullest. How do we get what we need out of this transitional moment and move forward with minimal regrets and a lifetime of memories?

To start, show up emotionally. Let go of all the planning you worked so hard to achieve and embrace imperfection. That sounds gauzy and hippy and impossible, right? Well, it's really none of those things. In this chapter, we'll lay the groundwork for the day itself: strategies for organizing the event, creating spreadsheets and timelines, asking for help, and then handing all that work to a wedding stage manager or day-of coordinator (or anyone who is not you). Once you've done all that, we'll discuss how to move from the planning to the doing. We'll tackle managing family drama and learning when to let go of all the stress and stay present. And finally, we'll discover how weddings are impossible to ruin, which is less crazy than it sounds.

ecce

What Happened When Our Wedding Got Snowed Out . . . in August

By Anna Mahony

We got married on August 15 and had planned an awesome BBQ picnic on a ranch in a meadow by a lake in the Colorado mountains. Think ribs, potato salad, home-brewed beer, and apple pie, followed by an epic dance party. Nice, right?

I say "had planned" because all of that didn't actually happen. Why? Well, two hours before the ceremony was set to start, it began raining. Then, an hour later the temperature dropped to 37 degrees, and it started hailing and snowing. Did we have a Plan B? Nope. We'd planned pretty much everything except a Plan B, because it's usually 95 degrees and hot as h-e-double-hockey-sticks during this time of year. Snow? That wasn't on our wedding radar. No way, no sir.

So. Our guests were set to arrive in fifteen minutes, and as Mike and I watched torrential rain blow chairs over and tablecloths away, we let go of the wedding we'd worked to plan for so many months. We decided to move the whole shindig

(continues)

up the hill to an old barn and hoped for the best. The most important thing was that we got married that day, and we were going to Do It or Else.

But here is where things got good. Here is when our wedding actually happened. Because when the guests arrived and saw us—wearing jeans and rain slickers—moving food, supplies, and tables up a muddy hill in the rain, they got to work. They created an assembly line to get chairs up to the second floor of the barn for the ceremony. Mike's brother brought the car over and started bumping music. The caterers moved all their equipment inside, set up the bar, and started passing whiskey around to warm everyone up. People hung lights, lit candles, and set jars of flowers (that were supposed to be for the tables) up all over the place.

I'll remember everyone laughing, helping, and pitching in as some of the most wonderful moments of my life. Despite the rain and the mud and the cold, everyone had a fantastic time. I think it's actually pretty amazing that the universe rained on our wedding parade. It encouraged me to let go, to sit back and focus on what was really happening—that all our favorite people were together in one place and that I was promising to spend the rest of my life with my very best friend. At that moment, I was able to see that our wedding couldn't possibly go wrong, because the most important things were so very right.

∼∼∼∼

Planning: That Color-Coded Spreadsheet Is Actually Worth It

The ability for you—and those around you—to be laid-back on your wedding day depends heavily on well-laid plans. As someone who has planned many events, let me tell you, the most relaxed events feel that way because the event planner busted their ass making plans and then making contingency plans. In my family, the story is that at the end of their wedding day, my mom said to my dad, "All those months of planning, and it felt like it went by so fast." And my dad rather pragmatically responded, "If you hadn't done all that planning, today would have felt like it dragged on forever." And *that* is not the kind of forever you're looking for on your wedding day.

Events with large numbers of people (and by large, I mean more than four) and multiple vendors (by which I mean more than just the officiant) need to be planned. That's the bottom line. The tricky part is that if you're like most couples, this is the first major event you've ever had to plan. And you don't usually get a full support staff as an engagement present—which is key for all good event planning.

But, never fear. The basic guidelines for planning an event are straightforward, and we are going to walk through them together. Marchelle Farrell summed it up best when she told me, "Let us be clear: unless you are an event manager, or lead a life quite wonderfully different to mine, your wedding is likely to be the first big event you organize and host. But when you get down to the nitty-gritty of it, planning a wedding is essentially taking a series of decisions and making sure certain tasks get done." And that? You can do.

Some people would read all of this and tell you, "And that's why you need a wedding planner." But you don't. Not really. You might want a wedding planner. If you can afford a wedding planner, you might decide it's worth it to you. But at the end of the day, you don't *need* a wedding planner. What you do need are some system of organization that works for you and a wedding stage manager to hand everything over to the day before your wedding.

The first part of getting organized is figuring out what sort of system is going to make sense for you. Some people work best with Post-it notes and piles of papers. Other people like wedding binders—everything in hard copy. Some couples fall in love with online all-in-one planners—Web-based products that you can even use from your phone. Me, I'm an old-school event-planner type. I like a good spreadsheet, and I'd argue that it's likely you're going to need a spreadsheet, no matter what other tools you use. Spreadsheets give you one central place where you can enter and sort information and share it with whoever needs it.

(And no, Pinterest is not a wedding planning system. Don't @ me.)

> We kept all of our planning documents on Google Drive, so we'd just write down notes and tag each other in comments whenever we had a free moment. Both of us were incredibly invested in the planning process, but we had varying amounts of free time during our eighteen-month planning period. It was great to be able to keep everything we needed in one collaborative space. One of the most helpful documents we created was our planning timeline, which helped us keep track of what we needed to focus on that month and what could wait until later.
>
> —Sofia LaReina, who married her wife
> in the world's most community-driven
> summer-camp extravaganza

Wedding Planning Spreadsheets

Here is a list of some of the spreadsheets you might find useful for wedding planning. Do not let this list overwhelm you. Remember, this is supposed to make your life easier, not more complicated. And don't worry, on your wedding day, you won't be in charge of any of these.

⇉ **Guest list and RSVP**—It's helpful to include addresses (physical and email) here.
⇉ **Tasks that must get done and the person in charge of the task**—This will also help you and your partner in the early stages of planning.

≳ **Contacts**—You may end up talking to more than a few vendors, and if you keep their information organized, it will be easier for both you and your partner.

≳ **Important information for your wedding week**—This should include flight information, hotel information, and so on.

≳ **A wedding "weekend" spreadsheet**—What are the events? What needs to happen to make each event successful? Who is in charge of these tasks?

≳ **Hauling spreadsheet**—What needs to get delivered to and from your wedding site, who is going to get it there, and when?

≳ **The all-important day-of spreadsheet** (see sidebar)

The funny thing about wedding planning is that when it starts, it feels like it's all about pretty stuff. But when you are finally down to the wire, wedding planning has nothing to do with style and everything to do with hauling. Who is getting the beer to the picnic site? Who is transporting the decorations to the venue? Who is bringing the leftover flowers home? A successful wedding plan is not about picking out the perfect centerpiece; it's about making sure the centerpieces land on the tables.

ℓℓℓℓ

Your Day-Of Spreadsheet

Having a spreadsheet that outlines your wedding day in exquisite, painstaking detail may seem like a stressful way to fill your time prewedding. But trust me, this document will be the one you treasure above all others. It will be the one that you hand over to your wedding stage manager or your day-of coordinator. It will be what makes the day flow smoothly, and the one that allows you to fully let go and absorb the experience

(continues)

of getting married, knowing there is a good plan in competent hands.

This sample spreadsheet is based on our wedding day. It's divided into four columns: Time, Activity, Location, and Person In Charge. I have included just the section of our spreadsheet pertaining to the reception, but I'd encourage you to do equally detailed planning for the whole day, and perhaps for the day before as well.

Time	Activity	Location	Person In Charge
10:30am	Ceremony starts	Venue - Outdoors	—
11:00am	Ceremony ends	Venue - Outdoors	—
11:00am	Yichud	Venue - Indoors	Meg & David
11:00am	Cocktail hour starts	Venue - Outdoors	—
11:00am	Polaroid duty	Venue - Indoors	Rachel, Wade, Amanda, Gabby
11:00am	Playlist monitor & Sound tech	Venue - Indoors	Kevin
11:00am	MC	Venue - Indoors	Emily
11:15am	A few couple pictures	Venue - Outdoors	Meg, David, photographers
11:20am	Meg & David join cocktails	Venue - Outdoors	Meg & David
11:45am	Toasts begin	Venue - Indoors	Stan, Various
Noon	Lunch is served	Venue - Indoors	—
12:45pm	Cake cutting	Venue - Indoors	Meg & David
12:50pm	First dance	Venue - Indoors	Meg & David
1:00pm	DANCE PARTY	Venue - Indoors	—
1:35pm	Chair dance	Venue - Indoors	Meg & David
1:45pm	Mezinka	Venue - Indoors	Anita & Stan
1:50pm	Hora	Venue - Indoors	—
2:00pm	DANCE PARTY, cont'd.	Venue - Indoors	—
2:40pm	Last dance	Venue - Indoors	Meg & David
2:45pm	Send-off	Venue - Outdoors	Meg, David, Kate
3:00pm	Party is over	Venue - Indoors	—
3:00pm	Flowers/Leftovers given out	Venue - Indoors	Kate, Caterers
3:00pm	Presents/Wine/Ritual items taken home	Venue - Indoors	Both families
3:00pm	Sound system struck	Venue - Indoors	Kevin, Kory
3:30pm	Items transported to Meg & David's apartment	Truck	Kate, Kevin, Rachel, Wade

ꙮꙮꙮ

One word of warning: while it's important to plan what your help-ers will be doing on your wedding day, don't try to direct your guests. Sara Hilliard Garratt, who got married after a four-day celebration in a

nature reserve in South Africa, put it this way: "Don't try to microman-
age your guests. Most of them are grown-ups (and the children are even
harder to organize). Micromanaging might be appreciated by a grand
total of five people, but on the whole, guests probably couldn't be both-
ered: they'll do what makes them happy in the context of celebrating
your marriage." The modern wedding industry occasionally has the bad
idea of treating wedding guests like props in a production: Have them
stand here! Tell them to wear pink and black! Make them open party
favors in unison! The fact is, your wedding guests are adults. They've
been going to weddings for a long time (many of them since well before
you were born), and they have a general idea of how to comport themselves. Allow them to do so.

Wedding Stage Manager: Nothing More, Nothing Less

While you may not have a wedding planner (and you'll do just fine without a wedding planner), you're not going to do this alone. Period. Every
time you get the bright idea that maybe you don't really need help, walk
over to the mirror and tell yourself, "No."

Wedding planning is really different from getting married. Or, as
Sharon Hsu, who married in a Presbyterian church in Atlanta, said,
"Planning the wedding was hard; getting married wasn't." Planning
your wedding is like planning any other event. There are contracts to
be signed, details to be worked out, a day (or more) to be scheduled,
and stuff to be transported. But on the wedding day itself, you need to
find a way to transform yourself from she-who-planned into she-who-is-
tying-the-knot. Don't even think of trying to do both. People who try
to run the show while getting married often turn into stressed-out and
scream-y humans. Attempting to do both at once is like trying to be

the stage manager of a play that you're starring in. You can't be worried about whether the caterer put the table numbers out when you're busy tying your life to that of another person.

What is the solution? I suggest picking a friend who will help you with day-of coordination, and calling this wonderful person a wedding stage manager. I like this term because it's no-nonsense, and it conveys the important task of the day: making sure it all gets done. A stage manager: nothing more, nothing less.

If you feel uncomfortable asking a friend for a no-strings-attached favor, consider asking a friend for a trade. Sara Hilliard Garratt explained, "Some people love to organize things. I know this because I'm one of them. Find those people. Use them, but insist that they don't stress. They will love it." Your wedding stage manager doesn't have to be your best friend, either. Don't force stage-managing on your most disorganized friend just because she will do anything for you in a pinch. You will be more stressed instead of less, and they will feel that they've disappointed you. Find the friend who is super-organized and secretly loves running things. Ask them to help and tell them that you in no way expect perfection. If they give you the gift of their organization for the day, and you give them the gift of your trust, things will work out well. Or well enough, and that's generally what we're aiming for.

And if you don't have someone you can ask to help, or you feel like you can afford it, for goodness' sake, hire a day-of coordinator (which is not the same thing as a planner and often is markedly less expensive). You are not failing in the unspoken chill-wedding contest if you get someone to help you out. Sometimes there is simplicity in paying someone to manage logistics for you, or it's worth it to have a hired authority figure to tell your mom to cool it. When hiring a wedding planner or coordinator, make sure you share a philosophy and that you like them. And for bonus points, hire one who's already read this book, so you're both on the same page.

ℓℓℓℓ

Your Day-Of Timeline

The average wedding timeline given in most planning handbooks is five and a half hours: half an hour for the ceremony, five hours for the reception. This is not always realistic, and it's certainly not traditional. If your reception isn't going to be five hours long, it will still be long enough. If you're partying long into the night, you'll want to plan for that, too.

No matter the length of your reception, it's worth it to plan the pacing and order of events. Successful entertaining is all about timing: feeding people when they are hungry and having one activity flow relatively seamlessly into the next. The more you're coloring outside the wedding lines, the more important it is for guests to feel taken care of. As long as you make it clear what is happening next, they will go with the flow. They might not even notice what you left out. Joy (mixed with organization) has a delightful way of blurring memories.

With that in mind, let's talk through things that you might want to include in your wedding day timeline (though obviously none of these things is mandatory). Once you create an outline for the day, you can turn it over to your wedding stage manager and know that the most important things will (probably) happen. Keep in mind: It's a wedding. Things are going to run late. Plan for that.

Prewedding Activities

- Getting ready—This can be together or apart.
- Spending quality time with friends and family—This is a nice way to spend the day if you are having an afternoon or evening reception.
- Venue setup—Try to outsource as much of this as you can to friends, loved ones, and/or professionals.
- Pictures—The more formal photos (think family portraits) you can take before the wedding starts, the more time you have to celebrate.

(continues)

☆ A first look—If you don't get ready together, but want to see each other before the ceremony, you might want to set up a formal first-look moment with your photographer.

☆ Getting to the venue—Make sure to schedule a realistic amount of time for this, accounting for traffic.

Ceremony-Related Activities

☆ Preceremony formalities—For example, a Ketubah signing, or any other traditions that are part of your cultural heritage.

☆ Processional—Make sure you allow time to get lined up and grounded before you walk down the aisle. Also, remember that you can opt out of a processional altogether, if you so choose.

☆ Ceremony—Guests tend to run late, so plan on starting your ceremony at least fifteen minutes after the time listed on your invitation.

☆ Receiving line—An official and traditional (but not mandatory) way to greet guests.

☆ Yichud—Jewish tradition requires that the couple take fifteen minutes alone together immediately after the ceremony. A variation on this tradition can be a wonderful way to soak in the enormity of what just happened, even for non-Jewish couples.

☆ If you have a legal marriage license, remember to sign it!

Reception Activities

☆ Cocktail hour

☆ A group photo of you and all your guests

☆ Wedding party photos—Hint: if you delay your guests' food so you can take hours of pictures, you will make them very cranky.

☆ Couple photos—Even if you take the bulk of your photos before the ceremony, taking five minutes of photos together when you're giddy from your vows can be wonderful. Consider taking more extensive photos before or after the reception, or even the next day.

- A grand entrance as a married couple—Very optional. Feel free to just wander into your reception if that's more your style.
- Toasts—As many or as few as you'd like, made by whoever is important to you.
- Food—This can mean serving a meal or serving snacks.
- Greeting of guests—Some couples formally make the rounds to say hello, which can be a nice alternative to a receiving line.
- Cutting a cake or other dessert—Remember that the cake cutting is still the traditional symbol that it's okay to leave. Make sure you have it late enough that you're fine if the older generation leaves, but not so late that the older generation wants to kill you.
- A first dance—This can happen before or after food.
- A family dance, a father-daughter dance, a mother-son dance
- General dancing
- Any ceremonial dances (the hora, etc.)
- Bouquet and/or garter toss
- A nondancing social activity, like board games
- A preorganized send-off

eeee

Asking for Help (Yes, You Need It)

Let me be clear: unless you are honest-to-god eloping, you will need help. And in this era of highly personal, very professional weddings, this can be tricky. When we asked our friends to help on our wedding day—to do things like help set up the flowers the morning of, or help run our DJ station—some people said no. More than that, people were slightly confused to be asked. Aren't weddings parties that you just show up to? Why would we ask them to help? But with some explaining, and many promised drinks, people stepped up. "I learned that some friends, while they mean the best, really just won't come through when you need them to, which can be kind of heartbreaking," said Emily Gutman, who married on California's central coast. "I also learned that other friends, whom you don't think you can count on, so you don't even bother asking, will surprise you with support, or manual labor, when you least expect it." It's the people who do show up, who lift things, solve last-minute problems, and fix your makeup when you cry, that imbue your wedding day with an unexpected richness. It's those people who make the whole process worth it.

Some people are good at weddings. In fact, some normally flaky friends will stun you with how much they care about your wedding. But other friends? They might be horrible at weddings. Maybe they have never planned one, and they don't know what it's like. Or maybe they are introverts who hate big parties or are uncomfortable with the idea of marriage in general. If you end up having friends who don't help out, or don't support you during planning, remember this: some people are terrible at weddings, but phenomenal at other things—like fun gossip, and making you laugh when you're feeling blue. And that's okay. But remember, after asking for help, it is equally important that you let people give it in their own way. You allow your family and friends to love you when you let them help. It turns out that weddings have their own magic, and many people want to be part of that. People want to lift you up. Your job is to let them.

Maintaining Control: The "I'm Going to Kill You" Moment

We tend to think that on our wedding day everyone will be on their best behavior. And they will, sort of. But you know how your loved ones act in high-stress situations? You know how your mom freaks out on Thanksgiving about having the table set just right, and you have a brother who's super-delightful but slightly socially awkward in large groups, and you have two girlfriends who don't really get along very well after the four glasses of wine they always insist on having? Yeah. That stuff is going to happen on your wedding day because weddings are stressful. The secret is, it doesn't have to matter.

Being the person getting married has certain perks—one of which is being given a free pass to not care. More specifically, you're allowed to think, "I'm going to kill you!" and then to think, "You know what? I'm getting married right now. This is not my problem," and turn around and walk away.

You're not going to be able to make everyone happy on your wedding day, and that's fine. Keeping everyone happy is not your job. For ten hours of your life, your job is to protect your own experience; your job is to refuse to get emotionally involved when people get stressed. It's tricky to just walk away and let it go, but your wedding celebration lasts for only a few short hours. Tomorrow you can get totally pissed at your mom when she starts berating your sister in front of your guests, but for today, it's not your problem.

You're probably going to have some moments of serious stress during your wedding weekend. Many of us have an "I'm going to kill you!" moment during the week of our wedding. That moment does not mean you are not having the proper wedding experience. It may just mean that you're paying attention to your surroundings and are calm enough to notice when the stress level creeps up.

The Emotional Bodyguard

You already have a wedding stage manager, but depending on the state of affairs in your family when the stress ratchets up, you might also want to consider getting an emotional bodyguard (and maybe giving your difficult stepmother one as well). Before you get married, you think that your wedding party exists to look pretty and throw you a bridal shower. Well, that's not quite it. Your wedding party exists in part to stand in front of you on your wedding day and not let drama within ten feet. Even if you don't have a wedding party, it might be a good idea to have a friend or two appointed to do this emotional bodyguard work. And yes, if you have a slightly irrational family member, assign someone who knows them well to the job of steering them away from the huge argument they were about to launch into.

Or maybe all of your friends and family are eminently chill, deeply reasonable, and never show signs of wear and tear under stress.

Maybe.

But you might want to appoint an emotional bodyguard just in case.

Letting Go: The "F*ck It" Moment

So, you had your "I'm going to kill you" moment. Maybe you even stayed up a little extra late on the night before your wedding, enumerating the people you would like to go jump in a lake, and are wondering if this makes you a bad person. Or maybe you had a calm night's sleep, with no stress, and woke up in a cloud of pink rose petals. Or maybe you were somewhere in between. Regardless, on your wedding day, you will move from the planning to the doing. To make this transition, you need to have your "f*ck it" moment.

At some point on your wedding day, all that doing must become being. If you have a hard time letting go of stress, I suggest predesignating your "f*ck it" moment. A good choice is the moment you prepare to put on your wedding outfit. You've done your very best to plan your wedding. You've done the emotional preparation for this life transition. It's time to let the rest go. Maybe your flowers are going to turn out just the way you imagined them; maybe they are not. Maybe your family members are going to be delightful; maybe they are going to get drunk and scream-y. At this point in the game, you can't control the outcome.

You can only trust that you did the best you could and that everything is going to play out as it should. Clare Adama advises, "There are certain images you get in your head of how you want the day to go, how you hope people will react and so on—hold these lightly and don't try to force them to happen. If you get so caught up in a particular part of the wedding happening a certain way, you will be disappointed and often miss out on how brilliant and creative the reality is." You are pulling your wedding dress out of the closet. Your wedding is happening. It's time to let go of how you wish things were, and instead tune in to how they actually are.

The No-Stress Deadline

Kimberly Greene, whose wedding came a year after her legal marriage, found, "For me, a nonprocrastinator who has to have things done before she can relax, it was super-helpful to have a no-more-stress deadline. Mine was two days before the wedding—after that, if something wasn't done, it wasn't getting done. And I honestly didn't care. It wasn't that kind of I-don't-care-on-the-outside-but-I'm-stressing-out-on-the-inside. I honestly just gave it up to Jesus. I mean, WWJD, anyway? He wouldn't stress about anyone handing out some program fans, I'll bet you that much." Once your wedding day arrives, the program fans might not get passed out, but you're going to get married. Start paying attention to that.

Embrace Imperfection

Theory: On one of the most symbolically important days of your life, you are going to throw a high-stress, high-stakes party with a lot of moving pieces; all of your family is going to get together under one roof with a lot of booze and a lot of emotion; you're going to make an important, weighty, lifetime commitment, and nothing is going to go wrong.

Practice: Things are going to go wrong.

There is a whole wedding marketing machine set up to sell you the perfect wedding, but the reality is, things are going to go wrong on your wedding day. That's fine. It's great, even. The imperfections make the day yours. You may deal with a sound system that doesn't show up, or a wedding dress that rips at the altar, or a venue that can't seem to get anything right, or a friend who does something hurtful. Imperfection is human and inevitable. So go into your wedding day expecting small missteps, and do your best to embrace them when they come your way. Crystal Germond, who threw a smallish backyard wedding, said, "Things weren't perfect by any means, but as my friend kept reminding me, beauty comes from imperfection. She literally kept telling me this every time I momentarily worried about food being cold or people not having fun or even flags getting twisted. She was so right." One of the gifts of your wedding day is the fact that you can choose, over and over again, in each moment, how you react to the things that go wrong. You can choose to allow the bigness of your commitment to take a front seat to the disappointments. "Perfect weddings don't exist," Anna Shapiro said. "People who say their weddings were perfect are people who made the conscious decision not to give a shit." Choose to let go, and choose to focus on the love filling the room. That is what you will remember in twenty years.

The Day Itself: Staying Present for the Whole Imperfect Thing

I'm not going to lie to you and say that being fully present on your wedding day is easy, but it is important. The key to fully experiencing your wedding day is surrender. The day is not going to be everything you hoped it would be; it's going to be more than that. And sometimes that's a good thing, and sometimes that's a hard thing. Because here is the honest truth:

Your wedding day might not feel like you expect it to feel.

After reading tons of wedding magazines and seeing zillions of wedding photos on Pinterest, it's hard not to have an idea of how your wedding day is going to feel. And that idea might be dead wrong. Anna Shapiro told me, "I thought I had a pretty good grip on how I would feel on the day of. I was wrong, and it is awesome that I was wrong. That is the beauty of it: the intense wave of emotions that swept over me, the desire to hug every single person that I'd ever met; I couldn't have foreseen it, and I just needed to, well, feel it. We can predict all sorts of things, like the mood we will set with our music and decor, but we cannot predict what it will feel like in that very moment, and we should embrace that."

Popular wedding culture has taught us to focus on our outfit, decorations, and details. We've all spent a lot of time planning how our wedding will look, and as a result we hope our wedding day is going to feel pretty and chic. The problem with this plan is that pretty and chic aren't emotions.

Trouble!

I'll leave you with this advice: it's really important to differentiate between how wedding pictures look and how your wedding day will feel. Our wedding pictures look dreamy and beautiful, and for that I'm grateful. Our wedding ceremony, on the other hand, felt intense, but not necessarily happy. And that was okay. There was plenty of time for joy at the party and in the weeks of bliss to come.

On the day itself, do everything you can to resist classifying your wedding day emotions as right or wrong. Maybe, like me, your life will change hard and fast, in a moment of gritty intensity. Maybe you'll ride a wave of joy, but at the end just feel like you threw an awesome party, nothing life-changing. Maybe you'll feel so overwhelmed that you'll weep for hours. Maybe it will be something totally different and even more unexpected. Whatever you feel, let yourself experience it. It may not be at all what you expected, and that may be a blessing.

> " Time stood still during the ceremony. It was like only Tere and I existed in the world, and the words we were saying to each other felt bigger than I ever could have imagined. It felt like the most natural thing, a ritual as old as time, yet also a privilege that we are both infinitely grateful to have, as marriage is still illegal in Panama, where we met.
>
> —Kelly Knowles, who married her wife in a binational lovefest in Joshua Tree National Park

Seeing Your Loved Ones: That Is Why You Are All Here

There is one profoundly good reason that you went through all the trouble it takes to plan a wedding, and that is because it gives you the chance to celebrate with your loved ones. The people who showed up to support you? Those are the right people. Crystal Germond described the end of her wedding this way: "Once night fell, we huddled around the bonfire and only went in the tent to get leftover food and pie. As the fire died, we threw our paper plates and wooden forks and decorations I'd spent so long cutting out with an X-Acto knife straight into the flames to keep us warm and together for just a little longer." The pretty parts of wedding planning are fun, but it all comes down to having the people you love in the same place, sharing the same moment. Luis Ramirez, who married his husband at Disneyland, told me, "A group of so many people important to us will probably not gather again until the last party that ever gets thrown for anybody, but we won't remember that one. That is the magic of a wedding." So breathe it in. This moment will stay with you for a long time to come and may end up bolstering you in ways that you could never expect.

The Great Thing About Weddings Is You Can't Ruin Them

If there is one thing you take away from this book, let it be the fact that it is really, really hard to ruin a wedding. Little things may go wrong, but you can choose to not let it matter. Susie Morrell learned from her small, funky Las Vegas wedding that "it can't be done wrong. It won't be perfect. You won't notice the chairs. Or the frozen margarita machine you paid for but never got. And you won't regret not doing something else. At least, we don't. When it comes down to it, none of that matters. You won't even care if your rings go missing." Fundamentally, you're there to get married. This is a huge and wonderful thing. It frees you from caring about frozen margarita machines, missing rings, and that detailed timeline you wrote, and allows you to just focus on the joy.

Beyond that, big things may go wrong. Emily Sterne, who married in Boston, had her outdoor wedding completely rained out, which turned out to be a blessing in disguise. She said, "I really think the rain bonded us all together in a way that wouldn't have happened otherwise. Instead of the outdoor location we had intended for our ceremony, we were married in our reception tent, with the chairs arranged so that everyone was in a big circle around us." The key is rolling with what happens and letting go of your dreams for the day, appreciating the reality of the moment.

It's possible that what seems like the biggest thing of all might go wrong: you won't love your wedding. Maybe you'll have fun, but it won't be the life-changing moment you expected. That's fine, too. "If you don't recognize a specific magical moment on your wedding day, it is okay. You have not failed," said Brooke Petermann, who married in Lincoln, Nebraska. "Maybe your entire day will be so subtly full of love that you just have to wait a few weeks or months for all of that goodness to accumulate in your postwedding brain." Or maybe you flat-out hated your wedding planning process, or something happened on your wedding day that left you in a puddle of tears. While you might need to mourn the wedding you wish you had, you still get to move on with married life, where hopefully each day keeps getting better. Nicole Lozano, who had a handcrafted wedding bash in Texas, put it this way: "Did I love my wedding? No. I don't think the stress that I experienced was worth it. Was it a great party? Oh yeah! Am I glad I got married? Hell yes. The other side rocks." And that is why you can't ruin a wedding. If you're marrying a partner who makes you deeply happy, the wedding just becomes the party to kick off the rest of your life.

Planning a wedding is such a giddy mix of beautiful things combined with a serious dose of pain in the ass, so it's easy to get focused on This One Day We Spent So Much Time and Money Planning. But that day is not the point. Your marriage is the point. So as your wedding day approaches, remember that this too shall pass. And what you'll be left with is your marriage, which is infinitely more beautiful than the most stunning wedding dress in the world.

My wedding day was one of the great joys of my life. But the happiest day of my life? That was probably a lazy honeymoon day with my husband, drinking whiskey and looking at castles . . . or meeting my kids for the first time. Or maybe it was just any old lazy Sunday, reading the *New York Times*, lounging around the house with my family . . . and, oh yeah, not planning a wedding.

WEDDING HOMEWORK

○ If you haven't asked someone to be your wedding stage manager yet, now is the time. I don't care if your wedding is next week. You need help. So put down this book, pick up the phone, take a deep breath, and ask for it.

○ Have you created your wedding planning spreadsheets? You can find customizable copies of all the spreadsheets I talked about in this chapter at APracticalWedding.com/spreadsheets. You need them, even if your wedding is fast approaching. At *bare* minimum, come up with a wedding day timeline and pass it off to your newly appointed wedding stage manager.

○ Set an official no-stress deadline, after which you will emotionally let go. You've just planned a wedding. You're about to get married. Those are two totally different things. Give yourself permission to let go of the planning so you can fully experience this transformational moment in your life.

○ Come to terms with the fact that things will go wrong, and that your wedding might not feel the way you expect it to. Remember that all of that is part of the process, and allow yourself to show up for the whole marvelously imperfect thing.

○ Mantra for when your approaching wedding day feels overwhelming: "It can't be done wrong. It won't be perfect. At the end of the day, we'll be married, and that's what this whole damn thing is about."

9

It Actually Wasn't the Best Day of Your Whole Life

The End, and the Beginning

Finally, after all that planning, the wedding ends. Maybe your wedding felt like it went by in a flash, or maybe it felt like it stretched out for eternity. But at some point it is over, and that's how it should be. Anyone who tells you that the wedding is the end has it wrong. The wedding is the beginning of your marriage. Megan Dunn described her reception as feeling like a "lovely afterglow" to the meaningful commitment made at the ceremony. Our weddings are about promising to spend the rest of our lives together. The party is an afterglow of that promise and the start of everything else.

Postwedding Freedom

You hear a lot of talk about postwedding depression, and it exists. You've spent a huge amount of energy planning a party, you've surfed an emotional high, and it's likely that you're going to crash, sooner or later. For me, that crash came in a hotel room in London, jet-lagged out of my mind, when I started crying about how I never wanted to forget the way the wedding felt. I was glad to be married, but part of me was sad to be moving away from the great joy that was our wedding. If part of your identity has, however momentarily, become wrapped up in planning a wedding, it's natural that letting go of that identity can be a little sad. Allow yourself time to mourn. The wedding is over; your life has changed; you are coming back to reality. Some crying is normal.

But there is a parallel phenomenon that no one ever talks about—postwedding freedom. Shortly after our wedding we were browsing in a bookstore, and I stumbled upon a wedding magazine. I looked at it, and I had this dull feeling in the pit of my stomach. Then suddenly I realized, "It's not my problem anymore!" And I felt terribly free. Because the truth is, on a gut level, I was glad that our wedding was over. It was an absurdly joyous day and an amazing party. But it was exactly the right length, and when it was over, I dashed out the door, giddy with the knowledge of what we'd just done. I was thrilled that our wedding had been so happy, but I was equally delighted that I never had to plan it again, and that I had the adventure of married life ahead of me.

When people say that your wedding is the happiest day of your life, they have it a little wrong. If all goes well, your wedding may be the happiest day of your life so far. But the wedding marks the beginning of married life; it is the announcement of the start of something great.

ℓℓℓℓ

Love That Just Keeps Growing

By Andrea Eisenberg

On our wedding day, after my father gave an uproarious speech, he pulled me aside and told me that there was something else he wanted to say in his speech, but he didn't think he could include it without being misunderstood. He told me that if there was one thing he was certain about it was that on that day, our wedding day, the day we'd chosen to stand in front of our friends and family to pledge our love and commitment to each other, that day was the day we'd love each other least for the rest of our marriage.

It took me a minute to puzzle that out, because I was bursting with love and joy that day. But once I understood what he meant, that we'd love each other more tomorrow than today, and more the day after that too, I told him that I hoped that was true.

Josh and I have been dealing with some difficult truths lately, but we are unbelievably fortunate to have each other every day.

I think back on our wedding day; it was only a year and a half ago, but what my father said is absolutely true. Compared to the love I have for him now, what I felt on our wedding day pales in comparison. I can hardly imagine the love we will share after decades of our life together.

At the time I'd thought our wedding day was the happiest day of my life, but I can't begin to describe the relief we felt the day after the wedding—when we were married, and we never had to do anything like that again. We could just get back to life as we knew it.

For a long time when people asked me "How's married life?" I always gave them my stock answer—"'Bout the same"—but, after a while I began to realize that wasn't exactly true. Little things started seeping in. When we fought, for example, even at our most vitriolic, things never really felt desperate—I knew that this fight wouldn't be the death knell of our relationship. We'd fight and then afterward we'd still be married.

We're a pretty boring couple, actually; we don't get out much. We like cooking, drinking wine, playing with the dogs, and gardening. We started looking at houses. I never thought I'd be such a cookie-cutter wife, but I wanted a house, and right around the time I turned thirty I started wanting a baby. Fortunately, so did Josh.

Something funny happened when we started trying to get pregnant. I noticed my body wasn't working right. I'd never really paid attention before, but now it seemed so

(continues)

obvious. I went to the doctor. The diagnosis? I am unable to have children. At first we were floored. We were devastated. We'd talked about adoption before we got married, but we'd talked about it the same way we'd talked about what to do if one of us gets hit by a bus. Could it happen? Sure, but we'd never entertained the idea that it was a real possibility.

That is, until it was our only possibility.

We took the time to grieve. To be honest, we're still grieving. I felt both betrayed and a betrayer—betrayed by my body and a betrayer to my husband, to our plan. On my worst day, I offered to walk away, to leave my husband so he could find a new wife, one who could give him the family he deserved. The look on his face told me he'd never even consider it.

It was that day that I really understood our marriage.

Despite our insistence to leave all of that in sickness and in health, in good times and in bad, and in joy as well as in sorrow stuff out of our vows, it was another one of those things that crept in unnoticed.

I don't have a heartwarming end to this story yet. We are still on our journey, still suffering, and still laughing together. But I feel like the tide has turned, and I think we will have our happy ending yet.

Even if it doesn't look like what we were expecting.

eeee

The Honeymoon: Time to Absorb the Inexplicable

The honeymoon is often marketed as the ultimate lavish escape: a time when you should spare no expense to have the perfect vacation. Because of that, if you're strapped for cash to spend on your wedding, or have limited vacation time, it seems obvious that you should cut the honeymoon and jump right back into life after the wedding. I'd advise against that.

For most of us, our wedding ends up being an intense emotional experience. Sometimes everything goes well, and you are over the moon. Sometimes you had to face up to difficult emotional truths, and you are exhausted. But after going through all of that together, you're going to need some time off, just the two of you, to process what just happened.

And the truth is you only get one chance to have the emotional bonding experience that is the postwedding honeymoon (though hopefully you'll have many chances to take fabulous vacations). The honeymoon allows you to bliss out and to try to absorb the magnitude of what you've just done together. Your wedding is a major life event, even if it's not the most important day of your life. Maybe you feel like it changes you in some intangible way; maybe your relationship feels exactly the same. But you will be tired; you will have the words *husband* or *wife* or *spouse* to get used to, new rings to stare at, and a party to talk over. So whether you jet off on an exotic adventure or just take four days in your apartment with an unplugged phone, take some time off, together. Think about what just happened. Savor being a brand-new family. Ponder the adventures ahead of you. Enjoy being married. And for goodness' sake, take a few naps.

> Maybe forever shouldn't be the explicit goal. Maybe the explicit goal should be in why we might want forever, and how to keep wanting it. What makes a relationship successful is not that it does not end—because hey. They all end, somehow. What makes a relationship successful is how much joy, delight, and victory you can wrestle from the jaws of a less-than-gentle world. Let's join hands and walk into that unknown with chips on our shoulders and swords in our hands. I'll take every moment with you I can have.
>
> —Harker Roslin, who got married
> and decided it wasn't forever

Toward Brave Marriages

Wedding planning is a trial by fire. It forces you to grapple with the tough issues: faith, family, friendship. It usually leads to some arguments, or at least some thoughtful discussions. And, no matter what, wedding planning forces you to make choices. Hopefully, this book has helped encourage you to say yes to things that are meaningful to you and a calm but firm no to things that are wrong for you. Hopefully you've fought through the hard parts and emerged on the other side with a hard-won sense of what matters to you and what doesn't. Think of this as practice.

Married life, and the family that the two of you just made together, does not have to look any one way. Married life is what you create; it's about what you dream up together. Sara Hilliard Garratt said that after she and her husband pulled off a wedding that felt like an uncompromising reflection of who they were, they thought, "Together, we could do anything we set our minds to." And so they did. After a lot of discussion about the life they wanted to live, and the family they wanted to grow into, they decided to embark on the wildest plan they could think of: sailing across the Pacific and exploring the Pacific Rim. And then, crazily enough, they did it.

For most of us, creating a family life won't look quite that extreme, but hopefully it will look quietly brave. Maybe you'll decide to travel the world together; maybe one of you will start your own business or go to grad school. Maybe you'll have kids young, or resist pressure and wait until you feel ready, or never have kids at all. Maybe you'll move to a farm, or stick with your tiny city apartment, or fully embrace the suburbs. But hopefully you'll make thoughtful choices with great grace, just like you did during wedding planning.

When marriage goes right, it allows us to be stronger people together than we would be apart. Shortly after her marriage, Catherine Sly said, "Our dear friend stood up at our wedding and confidently proclaimed, 'Marriage makes you free.' And I have no idea how he knew it, but he was right." Marriage allows us to support our partners to become the people they were meant to be. To empower them to pursue their dreams, and to live bravely and honestly. It allows us to live bravely and honestly ourselves. Marriage gives us the strength to continue to say yes to what is right for us. It gives us a foundation on which to build and the strength to dream big dreams.

Wishing You Love That Keeps on Growing

My wish for you is not just a happy wedding. My real wish is that married life makes you free, that being a family allows you to be your bravest self. My dream is that the foundation of your marriage allows you to offer support to your community in the same way that your loved ones offered you support on your wedding day. I hope that, on most days, you remember how lucky you are to be married to your partner. Mostly, I hope that you have many long and happy years supporting and loving each other. If that happens, your wedding was just a whisper of the magic that is to come. I can't wait to see what you create.

Afterword

I wrote the second edition of this book right before our tenth anniversary. Which is strange, because "tenth anniversary" seems like a huge milestone, not to mention a long time to be married. But if you asked me, I'd say our wedding happened just the other day.

But in the moments since only-yesterday we had two kids, built two careers, I wrote two books, and we lost two fathers. Oh, and we bought a house. But only one.

All those things I wrote after the wedding? About marriage making you free, and letting you create new things? For us, they were right on the money.

But I'm not here to tell you that my marriage is happy and intact ten years later because we did something particularly right. Plenty of the people that I quoted in the first edition of this book have gotten divorced. Many of them have also gotten really happily remarried. Some of them are happily single.

And that's the thing. None of us knows where we're going to end up, and to pretend otherwise is the height of hubris. Marriage is a collection of todays. It's today and today and today and today. It's waking up and choosing each other . . . and sometimes realizing that you can't make that choice anymore.

It's a negotiation. It's a living, breathing organism. It comes with good days and bad days, good years and bad years.

But if we're lucky, marriage is able to give us a foundation to navigate the truly hard parts of life.

Since I wrote this book, we've navigated more tragedies than I would have hoped for, and lost too many people, too young. During those awful moments, our marriage wasn't simple, because nothing was simple. But its consistency helped get us through. And the fact of the matter is that for us, being together has always been easy. Our relationship has always been something that pushed both of us forward. And in those truly dark nights, that showed up in just the way we needed.

But not every marriage looks like ours. And our marriage doesn't look the same from day to day, or year to year.

And ten years in, I'm mostly glad that we keep choosing each other, day after day.

Oh, yeah, and that my wedding dress was really stylish, too.

Selected Sources

I depended on the following books while writing, many of which I suggest readers pick up for further information, or just for delightful hours of reading.

The bulk of my research on the history of weddings in America came from the enthralling *All Dressed in White: The Irresistible Rise of the American Wedding* by Carol McD. Wallace (Penguin Books, 2004). I also used *Brides, Inc.: American Weddings and the Business of Tradition* by Vicki Howard (University of Pennsylvania Press, 2006), which offers an excellent exploration of the entwined nature of consumerism and American wedding tradition. I found information on the relatively new—and arguably faux—tradition of the unity candle in *One Perfect Day: The Selling of the American Wedding* by Rebecca Mead (Penguin Press, 2007). Beyond that, *One Perfect Day* helped guide my own wedding planning and wedding thinking, and it is a page-turning must-read for anyone headed down the aisle.

My perspective on all things wedding, and particularly wedding etiquette, has been unalterably shaped by the brilliant Judith Martin, whose Miss Manners books I have been reading since I was tall enough to drag them off the shelf (I must note that my parents, seemingly intentionally, placed them on very low shelves). In writing this book I have particularly depended on *Miss Manners' Guide to Excruciatingly*

Correct Behavior (W. W. Norton, 2005) and *Miss Manners' Guide to a Surprisingly Dignified Wedding* (W. W. Norton, 2010), cowritten with Jacobina Martin. If you haven't already read these, please do.

The way I approach wedding ceremonies was certainly influenced by the now classic *The New Jewish Wedding* by Anita Diamant (Fireside, 1985). Also, *Celebrating Interfaith Marriages: Creating Your Jewish/Christian Ceremony* by Rabbi Devon A. Lerner (Henry Holt, 1999) is the single best liturgical resource I've found for thinking about constructing a wedding service.

For more information on how the brain responds to choice, I recommend *The Paradox of Choice: Why More Is Less* by Barry Schwartz (HarperCollins, 2004). This book helped me make better decisions for our own wedding and informed what I wrote about planning here.

In this book I've also quoted *Emma* by Jane Austen (1816; Bantam Dell, 2004), *Pitching My Tent* by Anita Diamant (Scribner, 2003), and *A Jew Today* by Elie Wiesel (Vintage Books, 1979).

Acknowledgments

It is not lost on me that I'm lucky enough to get to write a second edition of this book, a book that was so ahead of its time it was unclear if I'd be able to find a publisher for it. "Nobody wants this," I was told over and over. "People want big huge weddings where they feel like princesses, and they don't care how much money they spend." That was wrong then, and it's wrong now. That's been proven by the nearly hundred thousand of you who have bought this book, scribbled in the margins, and passed it to friend after friend after friend. I recently had someone say to me that after this book had gone through five friends, they decided it was only fair to buy another copy. Nothing is a higher compliment. So, first among my thanks is for each of you: the readers of this book. Thank you for finding something that spoke to you in these pages, and passing that on, and on, and on some more.

Beyond that, books always take a village, and as ever I have a village to thank. Thank you to my editor, Renee Sedliar, for perpetually hashing out ideas over tacos and fighting for me to get a chance to make a second pass at this manuscript. Thank you to my former second-in-command, Maddie Eisenhart, for (among many things) collaborating with me on a cover image that nobody asked for, doing the original research and some of the writing on the article on my parents' wedding costs . . . and making the business run, and staying up far too late in the night to do it. Additional gratitude goes to Dana Eastland, who, again, stepped into my book-writing process in the ninth hour and helped with final research and so many little details. Also, thanks to Jareesa Tucker McClure, who worked to make sure I got the concepts around enslaved people and weddings right. And without Kate Bolen, this book would have never come to be, nor would our website be published while my head was in yet another book project. I'm also grateful to Rachel Wilkerson Miller for being my editor and guiding me through the process of publishing the article on my parents' wedding costs (updated here) as a viral article for BuzzFeed in 2017, as well as for being a badass and an inspiration to us all.

I could do nothing without my team and their enormous confidence and even bigger heart. Thanks of course to Maddie, who has led our team with an abundance of neon and glitter. I can't have enough gratitude for Chelsea Hanepen, our resident Capricorn, who keeps all of us on track, with grace and a will of steel. We could not function (or make money) without Keriann Kohler's mix of pragmatism and woo-woo vibes. Kate Bolen and Dana Eastland make sure our words go to print (and look good doing so). And to our one male team member, Mark Tioxon, who worked from his ICU bed in the last year . . . caring about our wild little project, even while working hard not to die (and blessedly achieving that goal). Beyond that, an enormous thanks to our team of writers, including but not limited to Liz Moorhead, Jareesa Tucker McClure, and she-who-cannot-be-properly-named . . . Amy March.

Getting your photo on a book cover is an exciting and stressful experience. (Nothing like knowing a whole lot of people who are going to see a particular photo of you for many years to come.) A great photo comes with a great team, and mine is the very best in the world. Thanks to Maddie Eisenhart for the photography, Chelsea Hanepen for her organization and tireless wind machine management, Yesenia Harbison for keeping my hair looking on point for the last seven years, Daniela

Saavedra for being the best colorist in the world (yup, I just thanked my colorist #notevenalittlebitsorry), Allie Yamaguchi for the makeup and vibes, and Butter& for making the world's best miniature cake.

In the years since I started APW at my kitchen table in 2008, I have not been able to express enough gratitude for our readers: the commenters, the silent participants . . . all of them. Our readers are some of the smartest, most compassionate, thoughtful womxn on the Internet. The fact that I get to be surrounded by the best people on the Web never ceases to amaze me.

When I wrote this book, all of our parents and my beloved grandmother were alive, and I thanked them all for believing in me. Since then we've lost both of our fathers and my grandmother. But even still, they all deserve thanks. Thanks to our families for their support, then and now. And thanks to my family for guiding me in person, and sometimes even in spirit.

Of course, none of this would have been possible without David, who is truly a husband among husbands. He was the one who told me, while I was crying (again) during the early days of wedding planning, that I should start a blog and call it A Practical Wedding. He believed in the project every step of the way, and insisted that I get an agent, write the proposal, do the work, write a second edition, and never give up. He makes me laugh, endlessly, and keeps me going, always. For all that, I am enormously grateful, profoundly devoted, and will forever be cheering him on.

And finally, to our two kids, who have taught me a new kind of love. Thank you for being your fabulous, dramatic, loving, over-the-top selves, and for supporting me wholeheartedly in everything I do (even when you don't fully understand what it is). You're my heart and my light, and I will love you both forever.

Index

About the Author

Photo by Portraits To The People

Meg Keene is the founder and editor-in-chief of A Practical Wedding, which started as a blogspot account on her kitchen table in 2008 and is now the top independently held wedding publication in the English language. Meg has published two (creatively named) books: A *Practical Wedding* and A *Practical Wedding Planner*. Meg's work has been referenced in the *New York Times*, the *Wall Street Journal*, NPR, Jezebel, and Refinery 29, among other outlets. She manages the best, most feminist team in the world from the APW offices in Oakland, California, where she lives with her excellent husband and two amazing kids.